ANNE
FRANK

BY DIEGO AGRIMBAU   ILLUSTRATED BY FABIÁN MEZQUITA

CAPSTONE PRESS
a capstone imprint

Graphic Library is published by Capstone Press,
1710 Roe Crest Drive, North Mankato, Minnesota 56003
www.mycapstone.com

Cataloging-in-Publication Data is available at the Library of
Congress website.
ISBN 978-1-5157-9161-4 (library binding)
ISBN 978-1-5157-9165-2 (paperback)
ISBN 978-1-5157-9169-0 (eBook PDF)

Summary: A graphic novel retelling of *The Diary of a
Young Girl*.

Author: Diego Agrimbau
Illustrator: Fabián Mezquita

Translated into the English language by Trusted Translations

Printed in China.
312

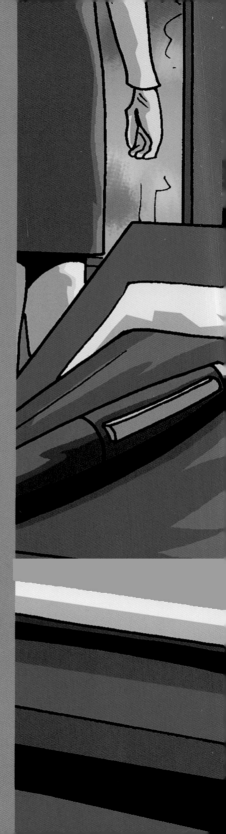

TABLE OF CONTENTS

Introducing

OTTO FRANK

EDITH FRANK

MARGOT FRANK

ANNE FRANK

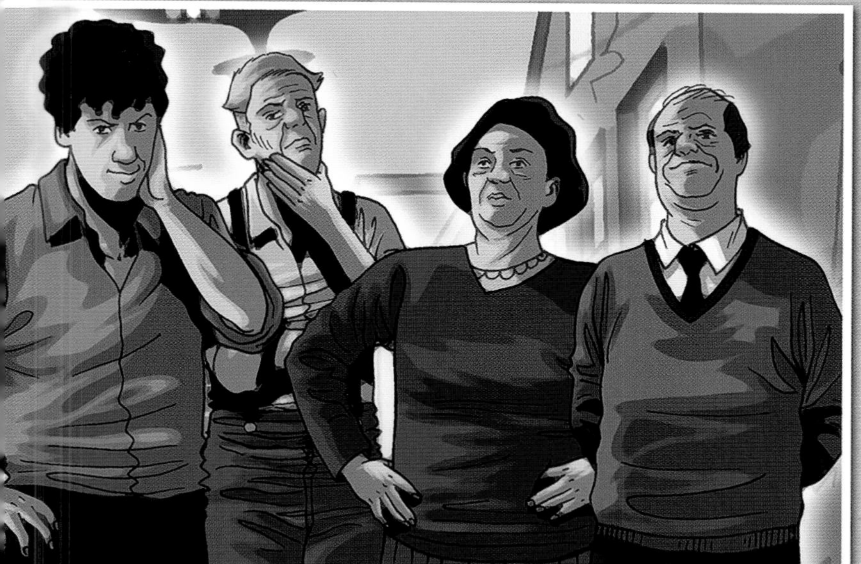
MR. DUSSEL
MRS. VAN DAAN
PETER VAN DAAN
MR. VAN DAAN

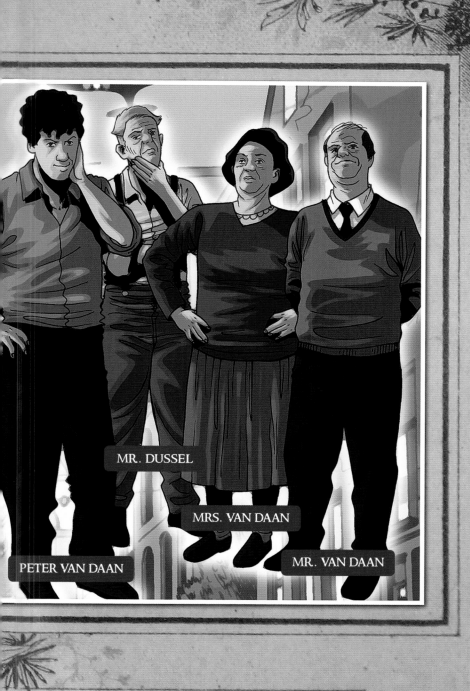

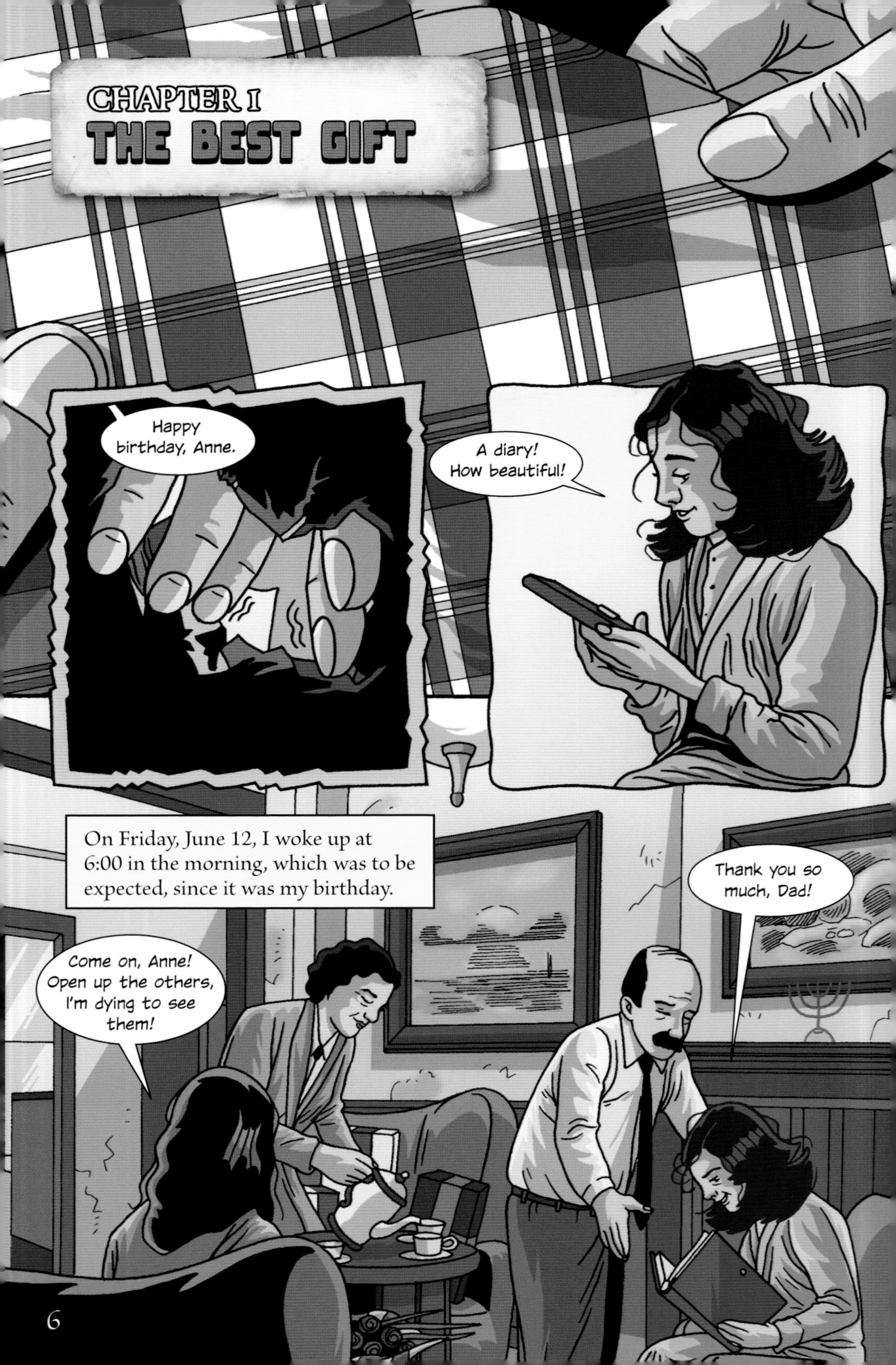
CHAPTER I
THE BEST GIFT
Happy birthday, Anne.
A diary! How beautiful!
On Friday, June 12, I woke up at 6:00 in the morning, which was to be expected, since it was my birthday.
Thank you so much, Dad!
Come on, Anne! Open up the others, I'm dying to see them!

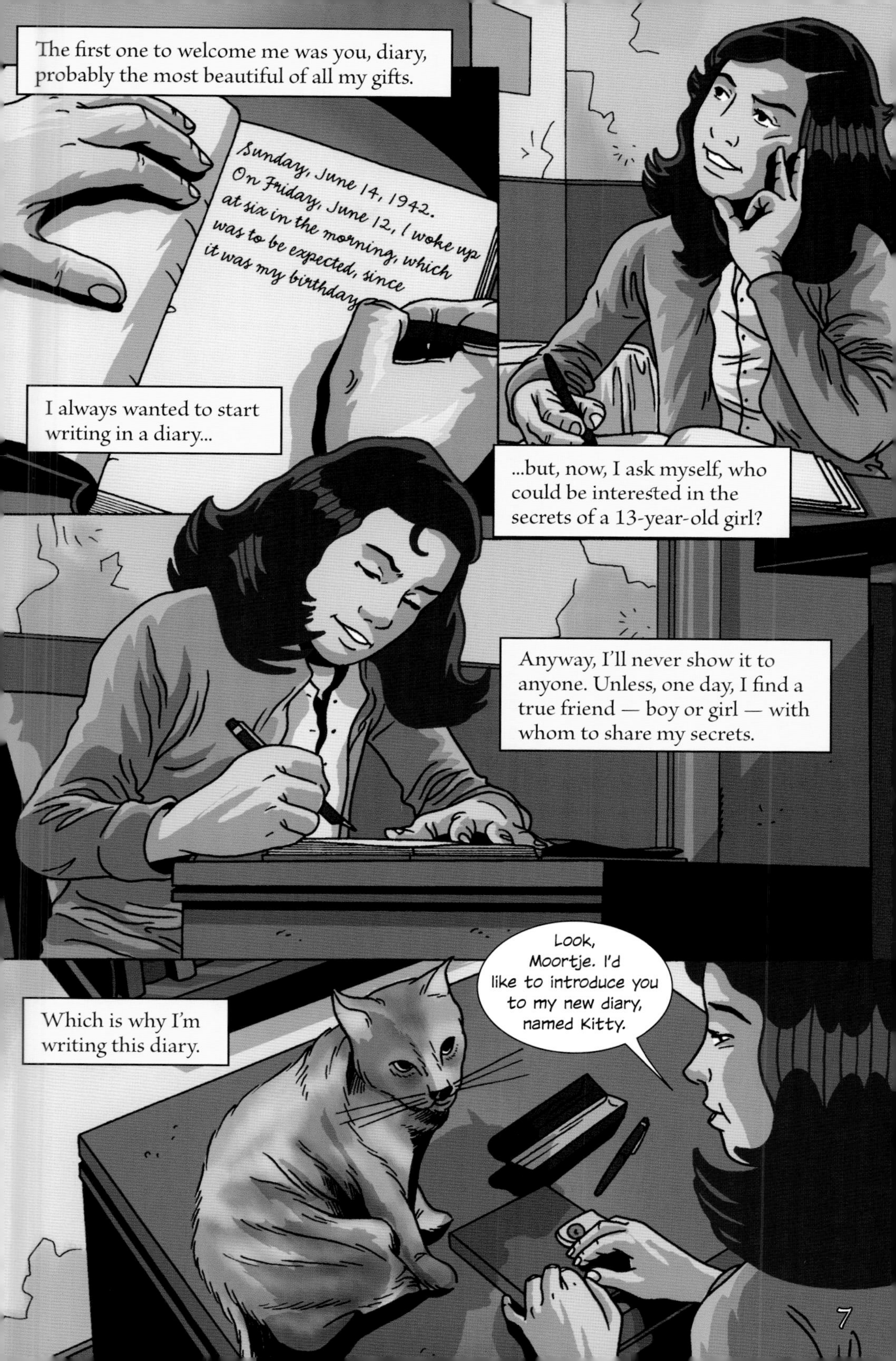

The first one to welcome me was you, diary, probably the most beautiful of all my gifts.
Sunday, June 14, 1942. On Friday, June 12, I woke up at six in the morning, which was to be expected, since it was my birthday
I always wanted to start writing in a diary...
...but, now, I ask myself, who could be interested in the secrets of a 13-year-old girl?
Anyway, I'll never show it to anyone. Unless, one day, I find a true friend — boy or girl — with whom to share my secrets.
Which is why I'm writing this diary.
Look, Moortje. I'd like to introduce you to my new diary, named Kitty.

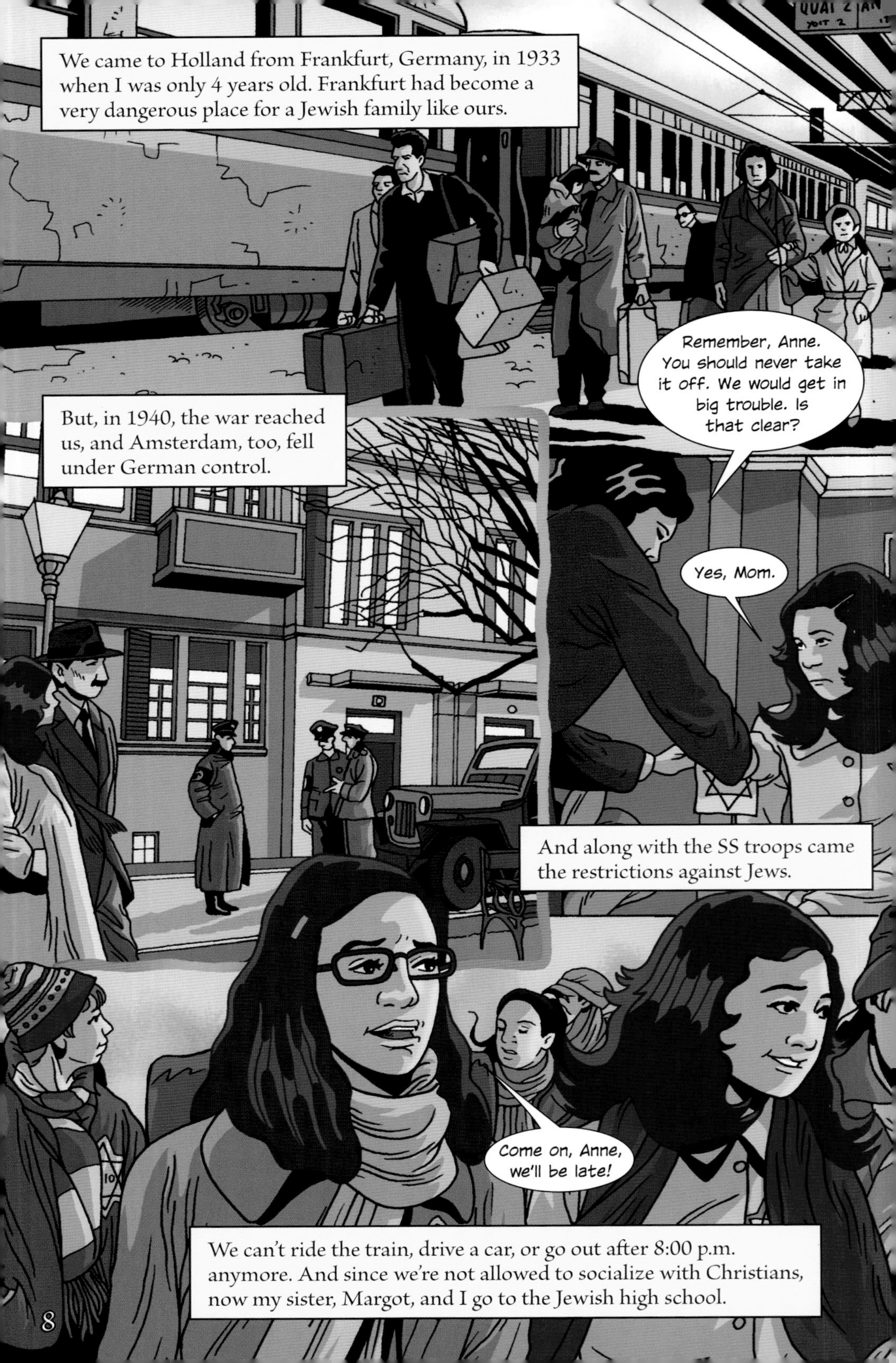
We came to Holland from Frankfurt, Germany, in 1933 when I was only 4 years old. Frankfurt had become a very dangerous place for a Jewish family like ours.
But, in 1940, the war reached us, and Amsterdam, too, fell under German control.
Remember, Anne. You should never take it off. We would get in big trouble. Is that clear?
Yes, Mom.
And along with the SS troops came the restrictions against Jews.
Come on, Anne, we'll be late!
We can't ride the train, drive a car, or go out after 8:00 p.m. anymore. And since we're not allowed to socialize with Christians, now my sister, Margot, and I go to the Jewish high school.

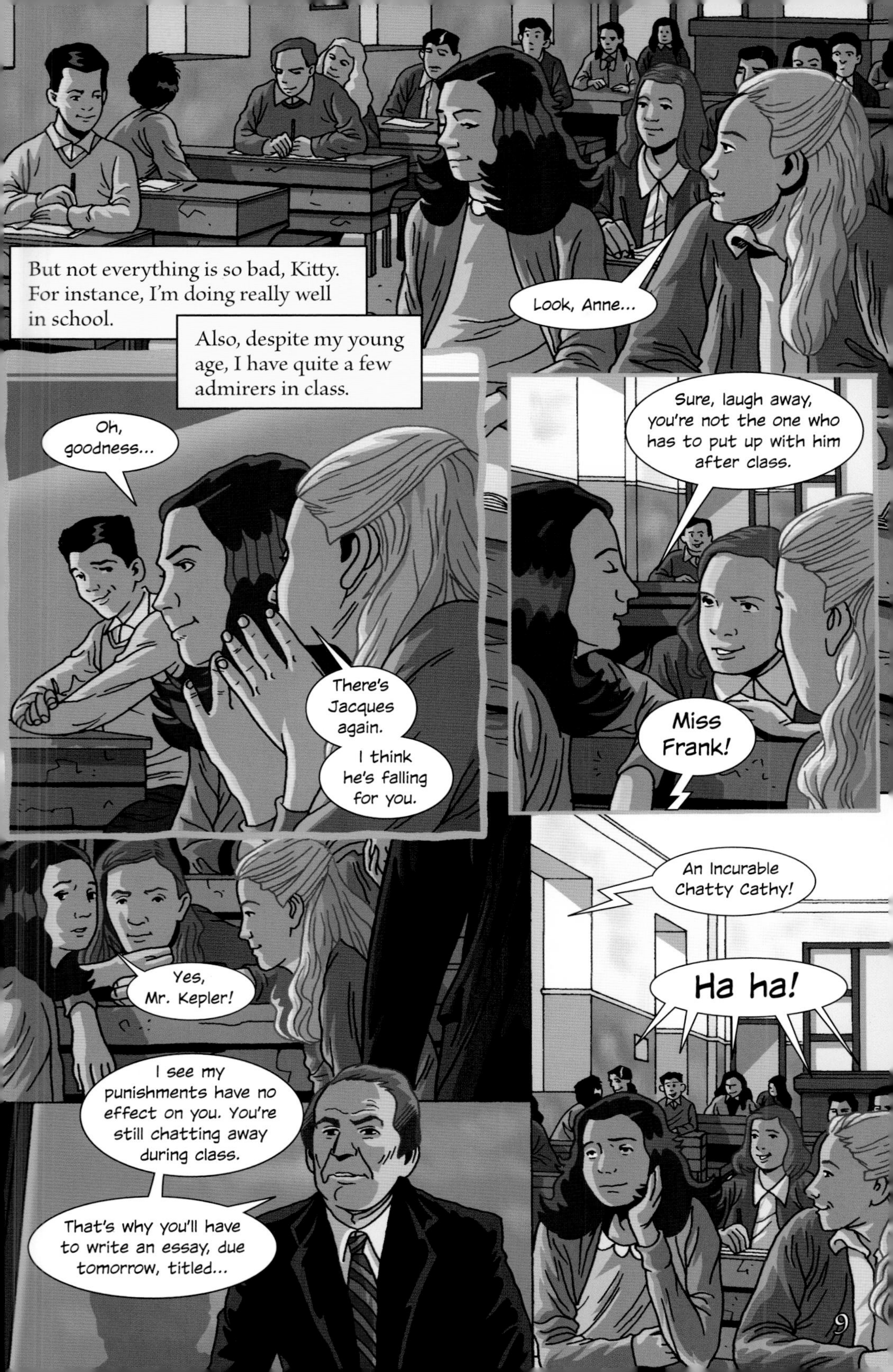

But not everything is so bad, Kitty. For instance, I'm doing really well in school.
Look, Anne...
Also, despite my young age, I have quite a few admirers in class.
Oh, goodness...
There's Jacques again.
I think he's falling for you.
Sure, laugh away, you're not the one who has to put up with him after class.
Miss Frank!
Yes, Mr. Kepler!
I see my punishments have no effect on you. You're still chatting away during class.
That's why you'll have to write an essay, due tomorrow, titled...
An Incurable Chatty Cathy!
Ha ha!

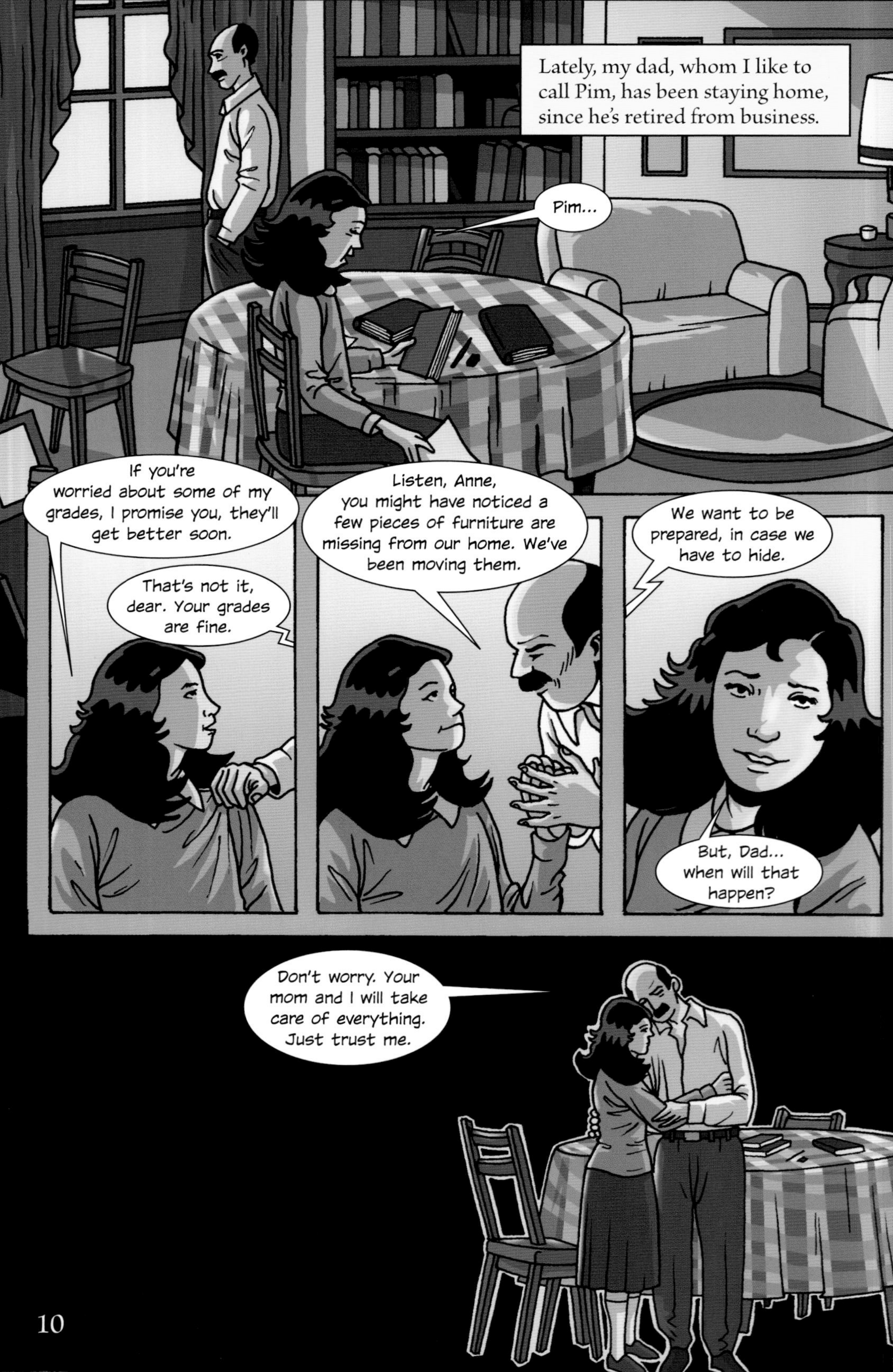
Lately, my dad, whom I like to call Pim, has been staying home, since he's retired from business.
Pim...
If you're worried about some of my grades, I promise you, they'll get better soon.
That's not it, dear. Your grades are fine.
Listen, Anne, you might have noticed a few pieces of furniture are missing from our home. We've been moving them.
We want to be prepared, in case we have to hide.
But, Dad... when will that happen?
Don't worry. Your mom and I will take care of everything. Just trust me.

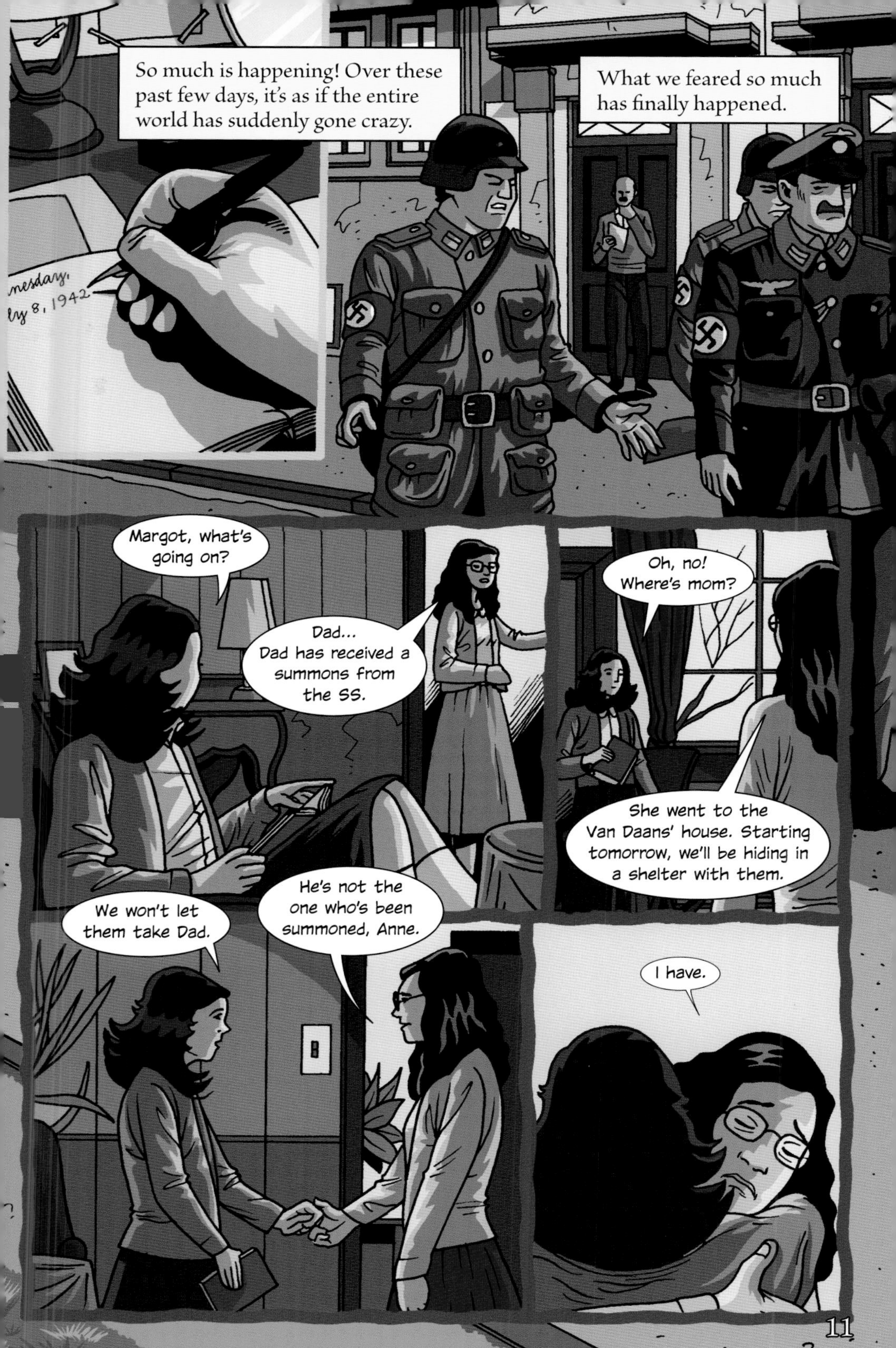

So much is happening! Over these past few days, it's as if the entire world has suddenly gone crazy.
nesday, ly 8, 1942
What we feared so much has finally happened.
Margot, what's going on?
Dad... Dad has received a summons from the SS.
Oh, no! Where's mom?
She went to the Van Daans' house. Starting tomorrow, we'll be hiding in a shelter with them.
We won't let them take Dad.
He's not the one who's been summoned, Anne.
I have.

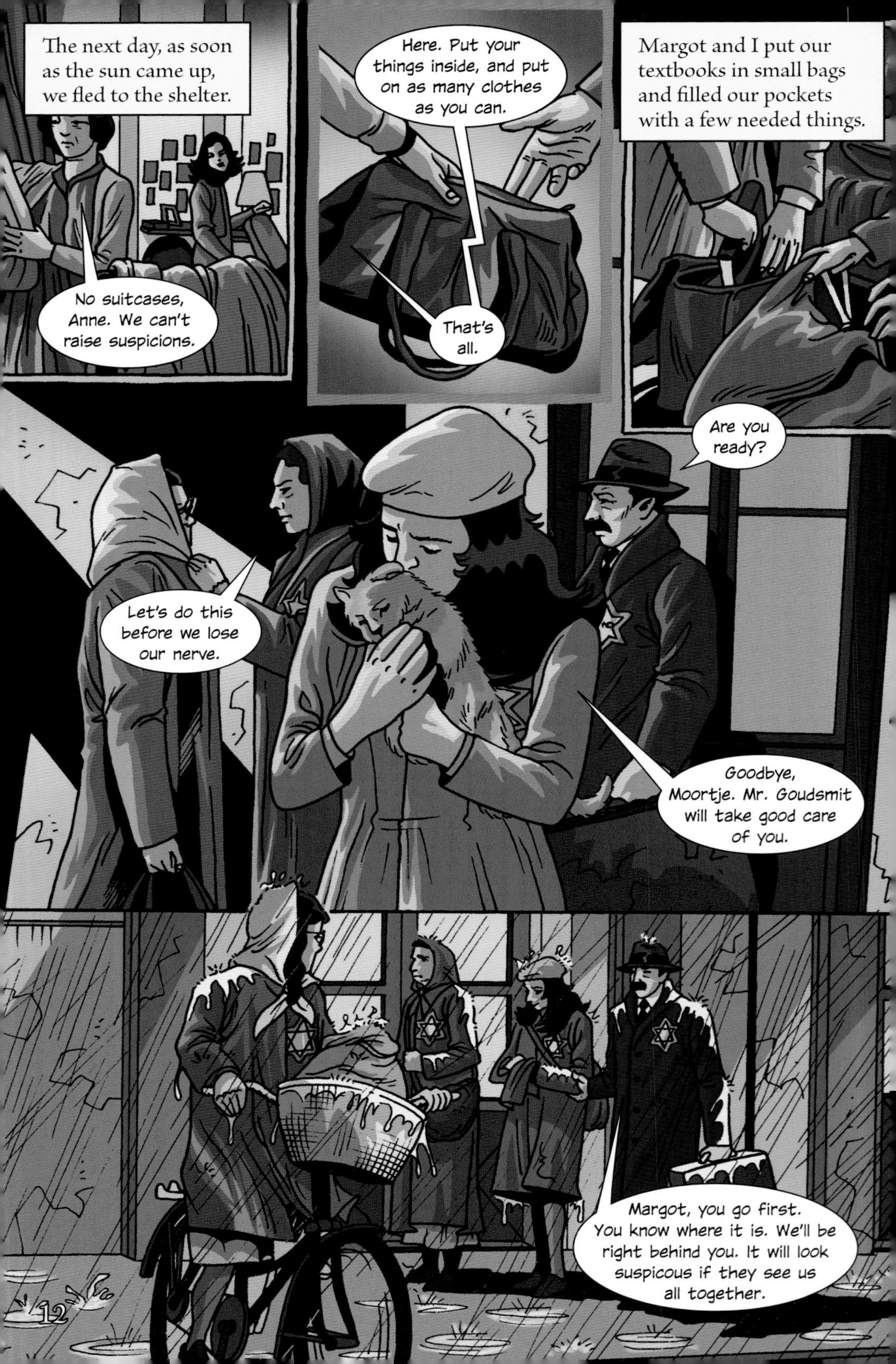
The next day, as soon as the sun came up, we fled to the shelter.
No suitcases, Anne. We can't raise suspicions.
Here. Put your things inside, and put on as many clothes as you can.
That's all.
Margot and I put our textbooks in small bags and filled our pockets with a few needed things.
Are you ready?
Let's do this before we lose our nerve.
Goodbye, Moortje. Mr. Goudsmit will take good care of you.
Margot, you go first. You know where it is. We'll be right behind you. It will look suspicous if they see us all together.

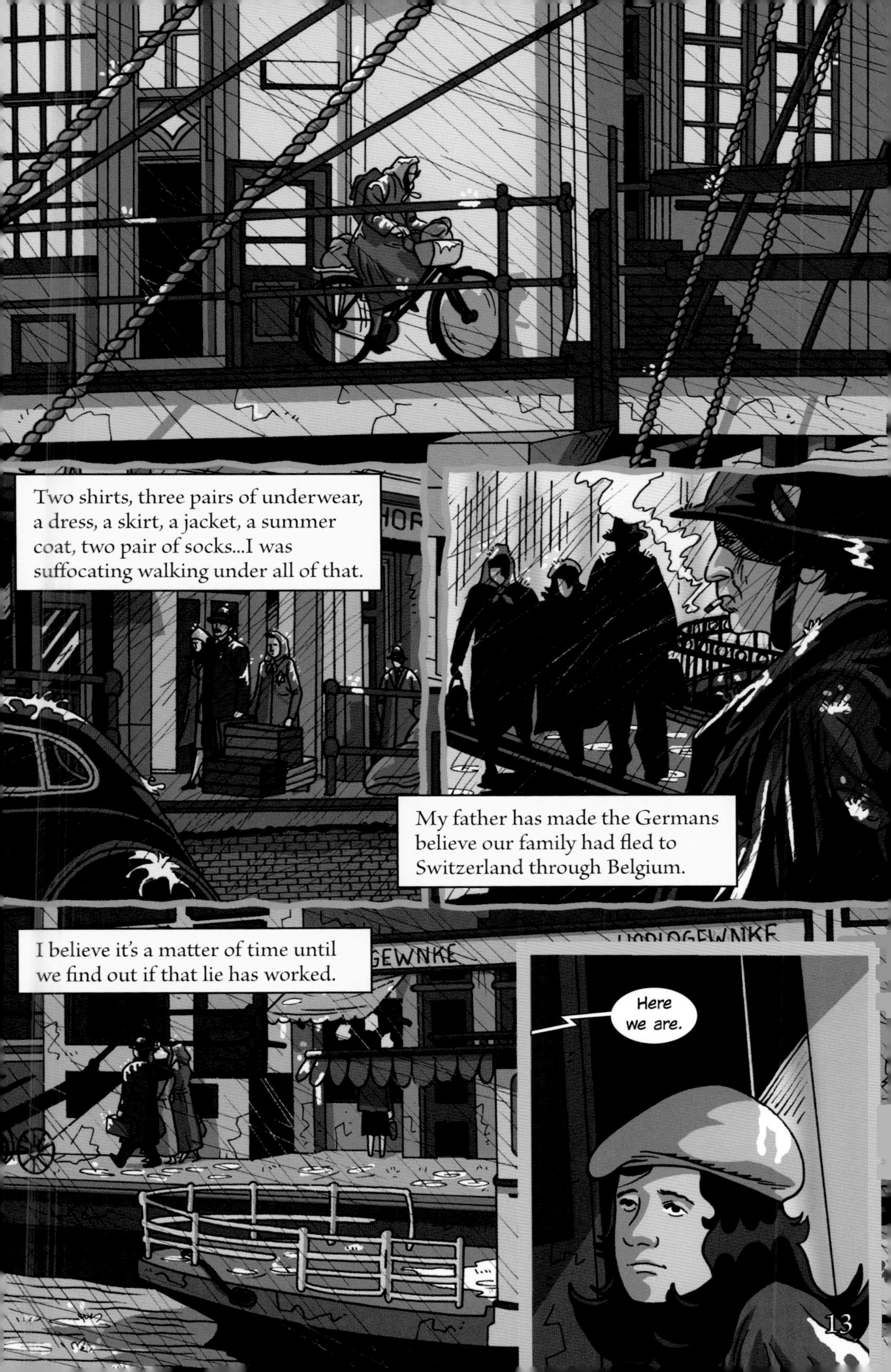

Two shirts, three pairs of underwear, a dress, a skirt, a jacket, a summer coat, two pair of socks...I was suffocating walking under all of that.
My father has made the Germans believe our family had fled to Switzerland through Belgium.
I believe it's a matter of time until we find out if that lie has worked.
Here we are.

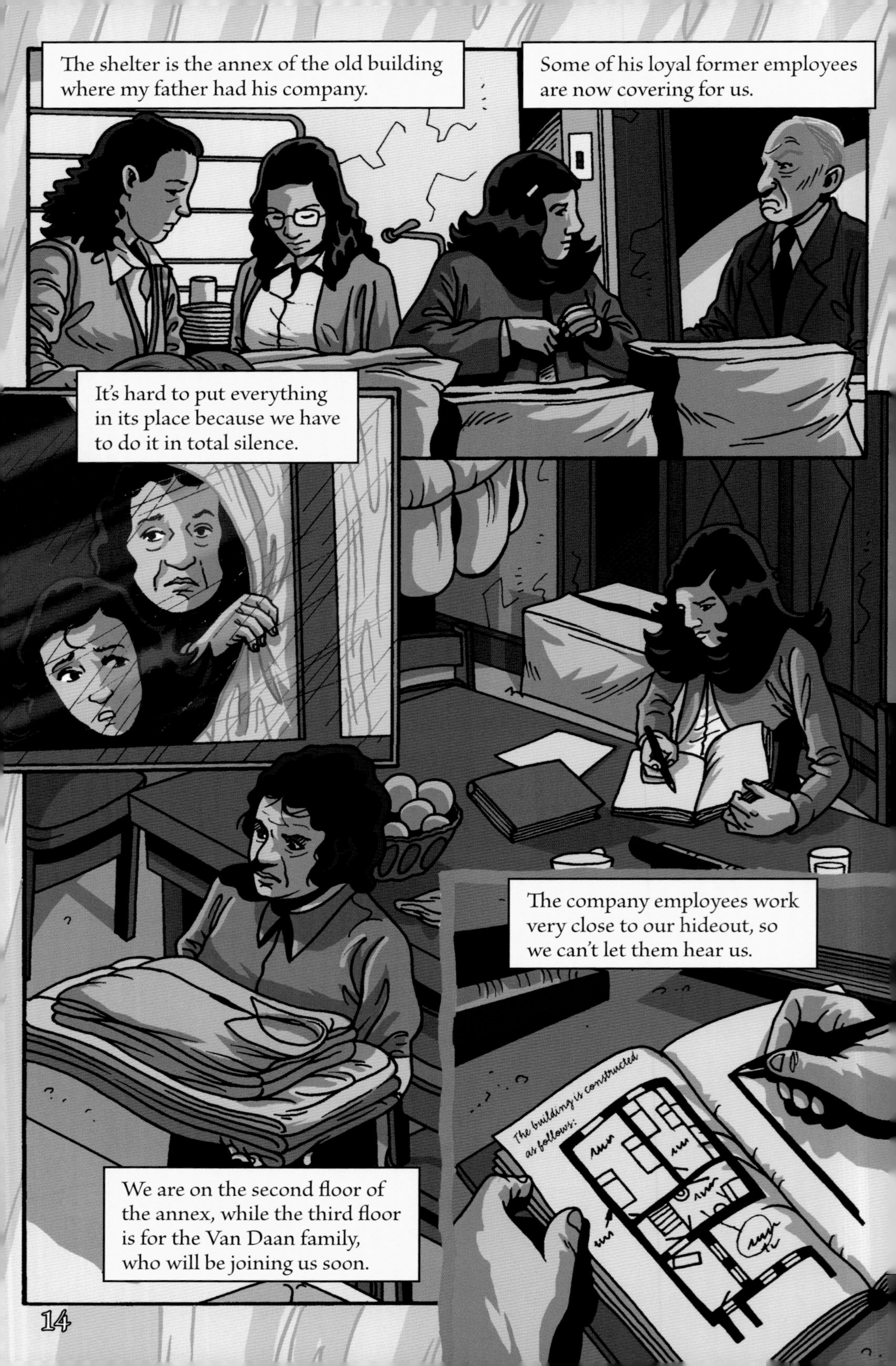
The shelter is the annex of the old building where my father had his company.
Some of his loyal former employees are now covering for us.
It's hard to put everything in its place because we have to do it in total silence.
The company employees work very close to our hideout, so we can't let them hear us.
The building is constructed as follows:
We are on the second floor of the annex, while the third floor is for the Van Daan family, who will be joining us soon.

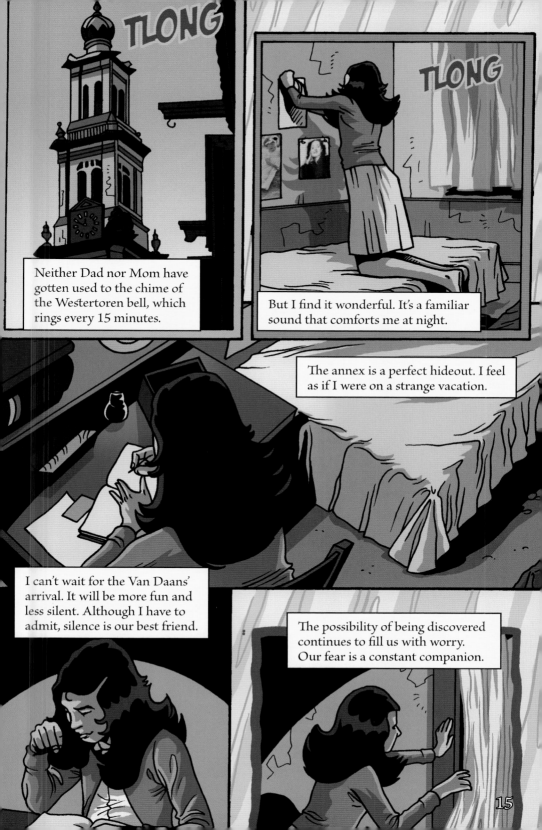

TLONG

Neither Dad nor Mom have gotten used to the chime of the Westertoren bell, which rings every 15 minutes.

TLONG

But I find it wonderful. It's a familiar sound that comforts me at night.

The annex is a perfect hideout. I feel as if I were on a strange vacation.

I can't wait for the Van Daans' arrival. It will be more fun and less silent. Although I have to admit, silence is our best friend.

The possibility of being discovered continues to fill us with worry. Our fear is a constant companion.

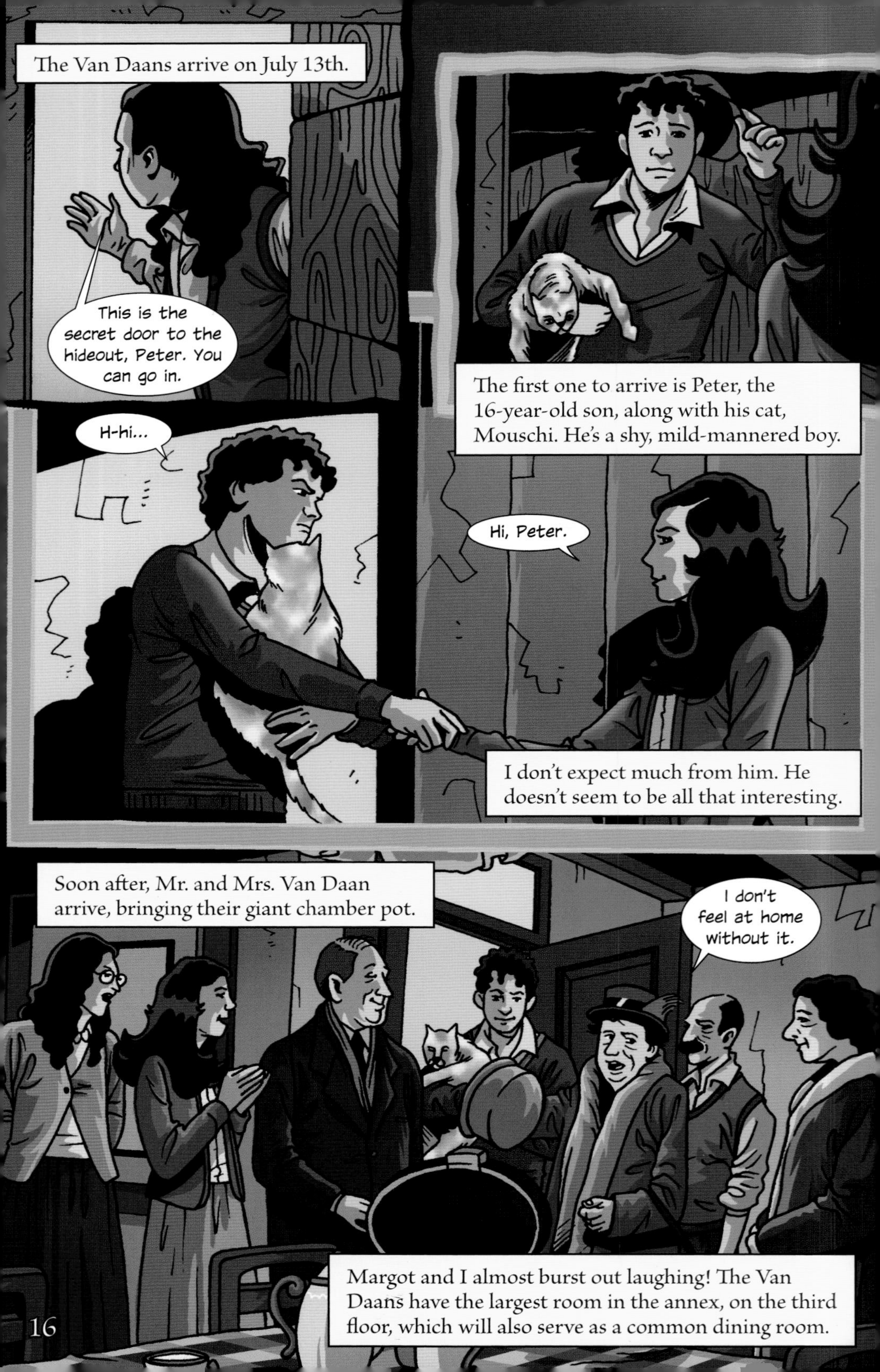
The Van Daans arrive on July 13th.
This is the secret door to the hideout, Peter. You can go in.
The first one to arrive is Peter, the 16-year-old son, along with his cat, Mouschi. He's a shy, mild-mannered boy.
H-hi...
Hi, Peter.
I don't expect much from him. He doesn't seem to be all that interesting.
Soon after, Mr. and Mrs. Van Daan arrive, bringing their giant chamber pot.
I don't feel at home without it.
Margot and I almost burst out laughing! The Van Daans have the largest room in the annex, on the third floor, which will also serve as a common dining room.

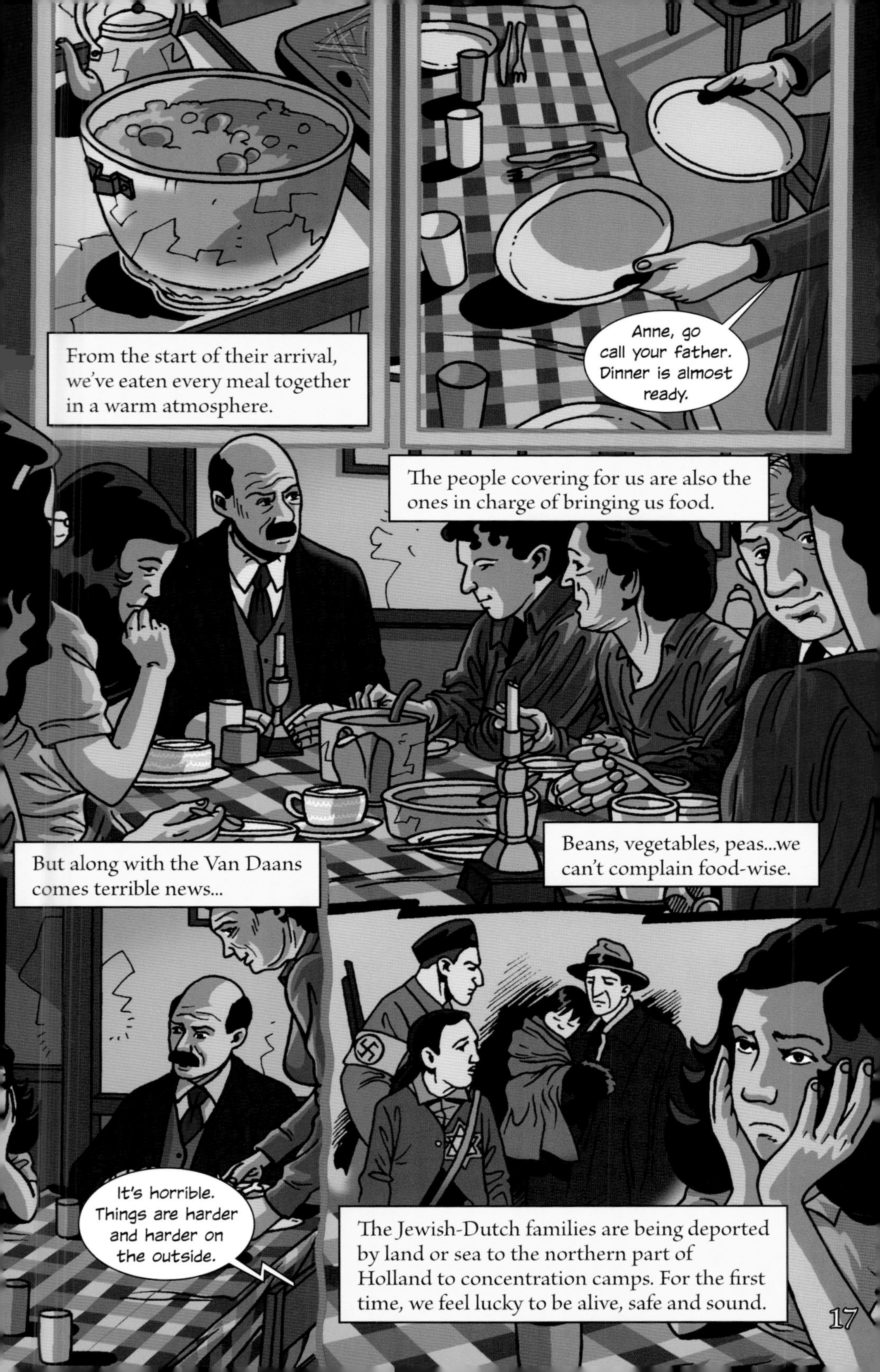
From the start of their arrival, we've eaten every meal together in a warm atmosphere.
Anne, go call your father. Dinner is almost ready.
The people covering for us are also the ones in charge of bringing us food.
Beans, vegetables, peas...we can't complain food-wise.
But along with the Van Daans comes terrible news...
It's horrible. Things are harder and harder on the outside.
The Jewish-Dutch families are being deported by land or sea to the northern part of Holland to concentration camps. For the first time, we feel lucky to be alive, safe and sound.

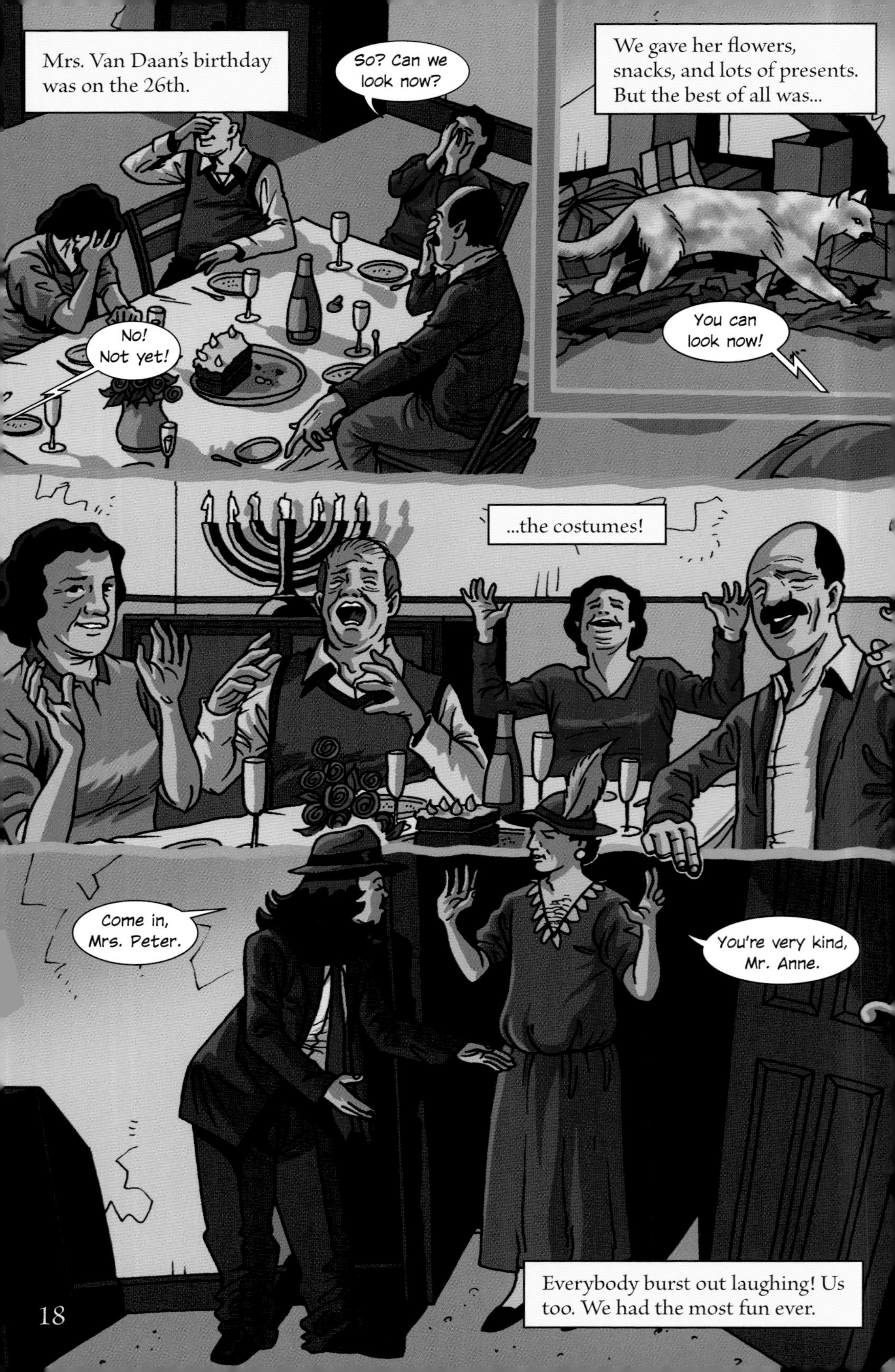
Mrs. Van Daan's birthday was on the 26th.
So? Can we look now?
No! Not yet!
We gave her flowers, snacks, and lots of presents. But the best of all was...
You can look now!
...the costumes!
Come in, Mrs. Peter.
You're very kind, Mr. Anne.
Everybody burst out laughing! Us too. We had the most fun ever.

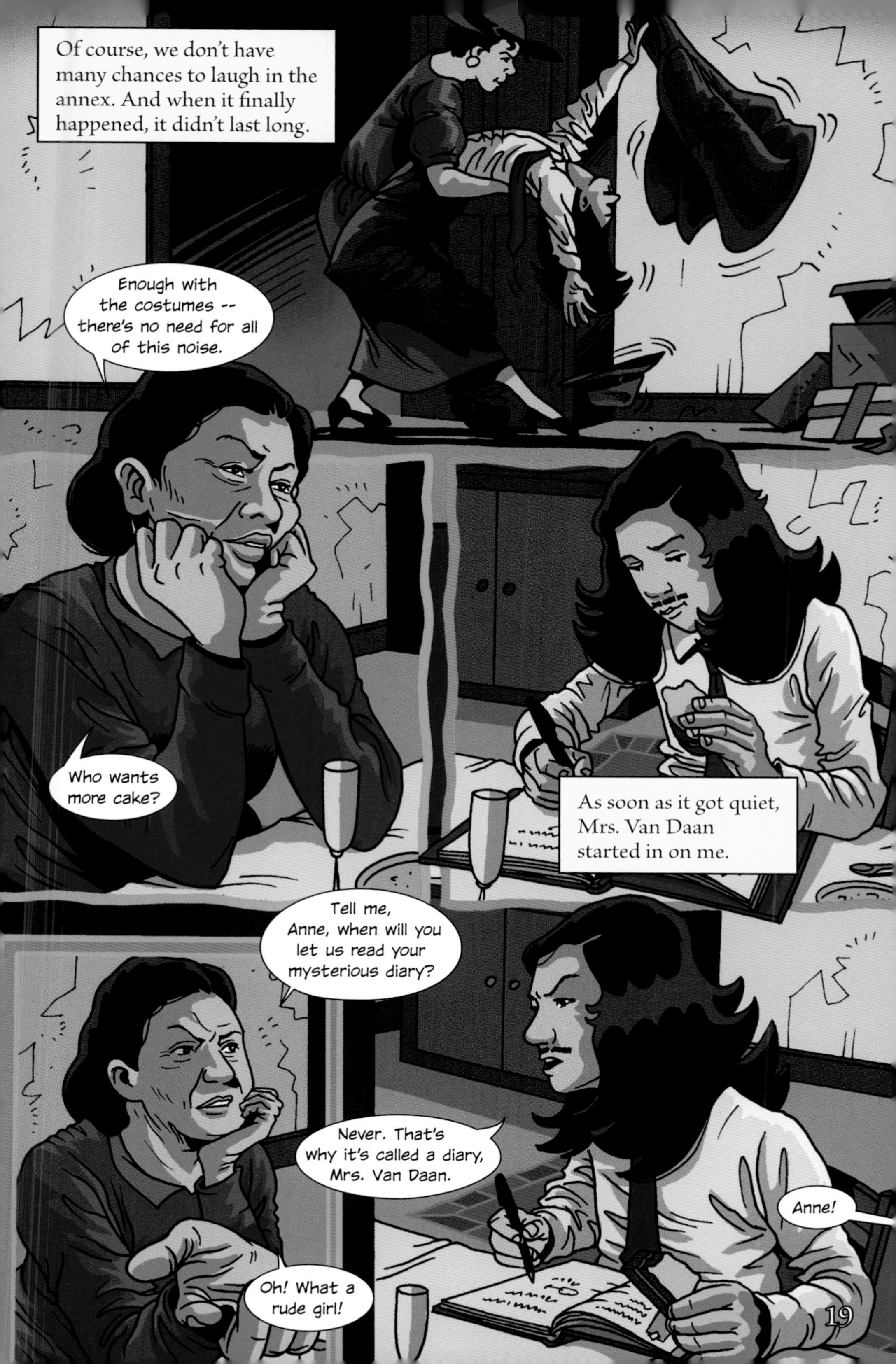

Of course, we don't have many chances to laugh in the annex. And when it finally happened, it didn't last long.
Enough with the costumes -- there's no need for all of this noise.
Who wants more cake?
As soon as it got quiet, Mrs. Van Daan started in on me.
Tell me, Anne, when will you let us read your mysterious diary?
Never. That's why it's called a diary, Mrs. Van Daan.
Anne!
Oh! What a rude girl!

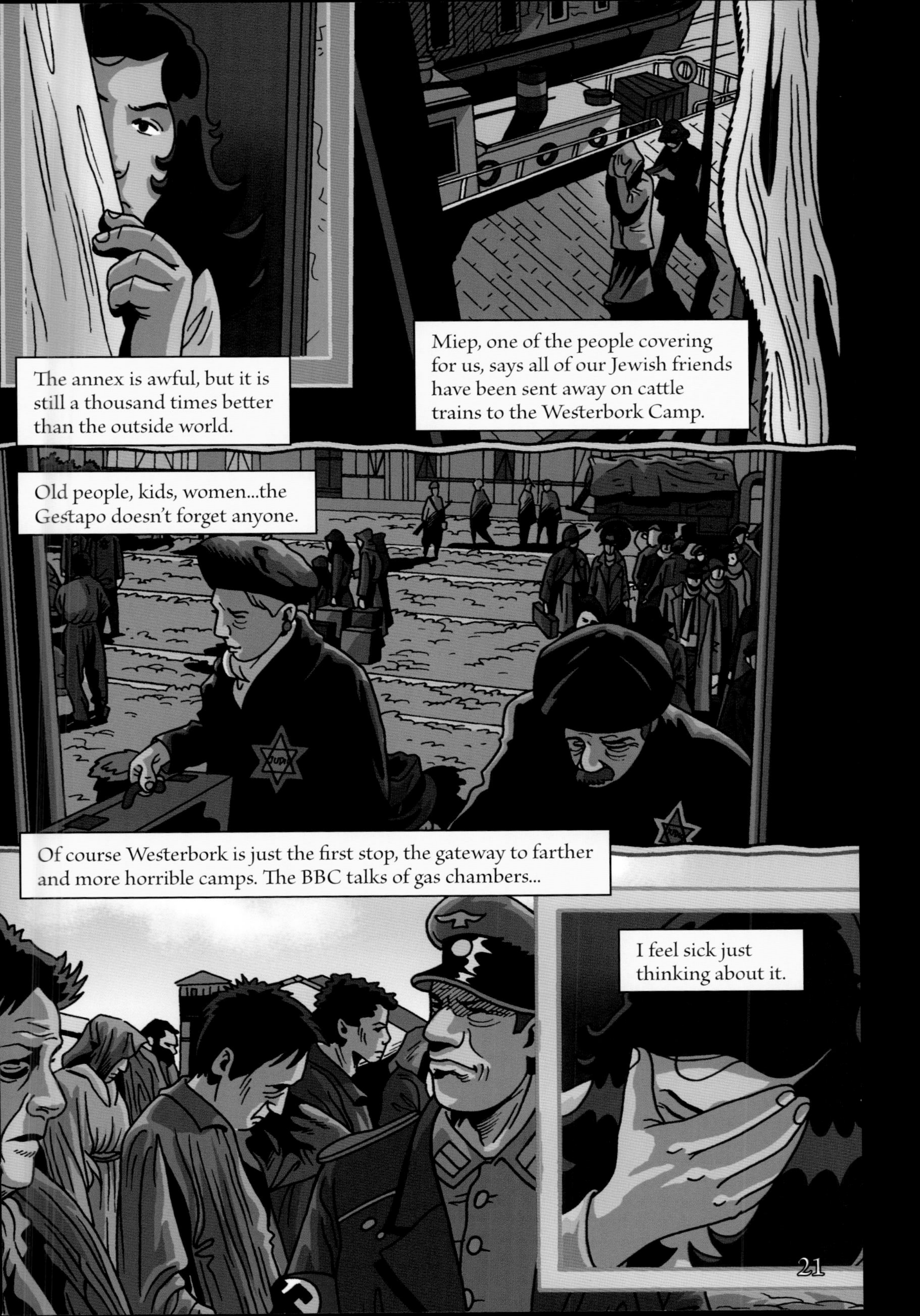

The annex is awful, but it is still a thousand times better than the outside world.
Miep, one of the people covering for us, says all of our Jewish friends have been sent away on cattle trains to the Westerbork Camp.
Old people, kids, women...the Gestapo doesn't forget anyone.
Of course Westerbork is just the first stop, the gateway to farther and more horrible camps. The BBC talks of gas chambers...
I feel sick just thinking about it.

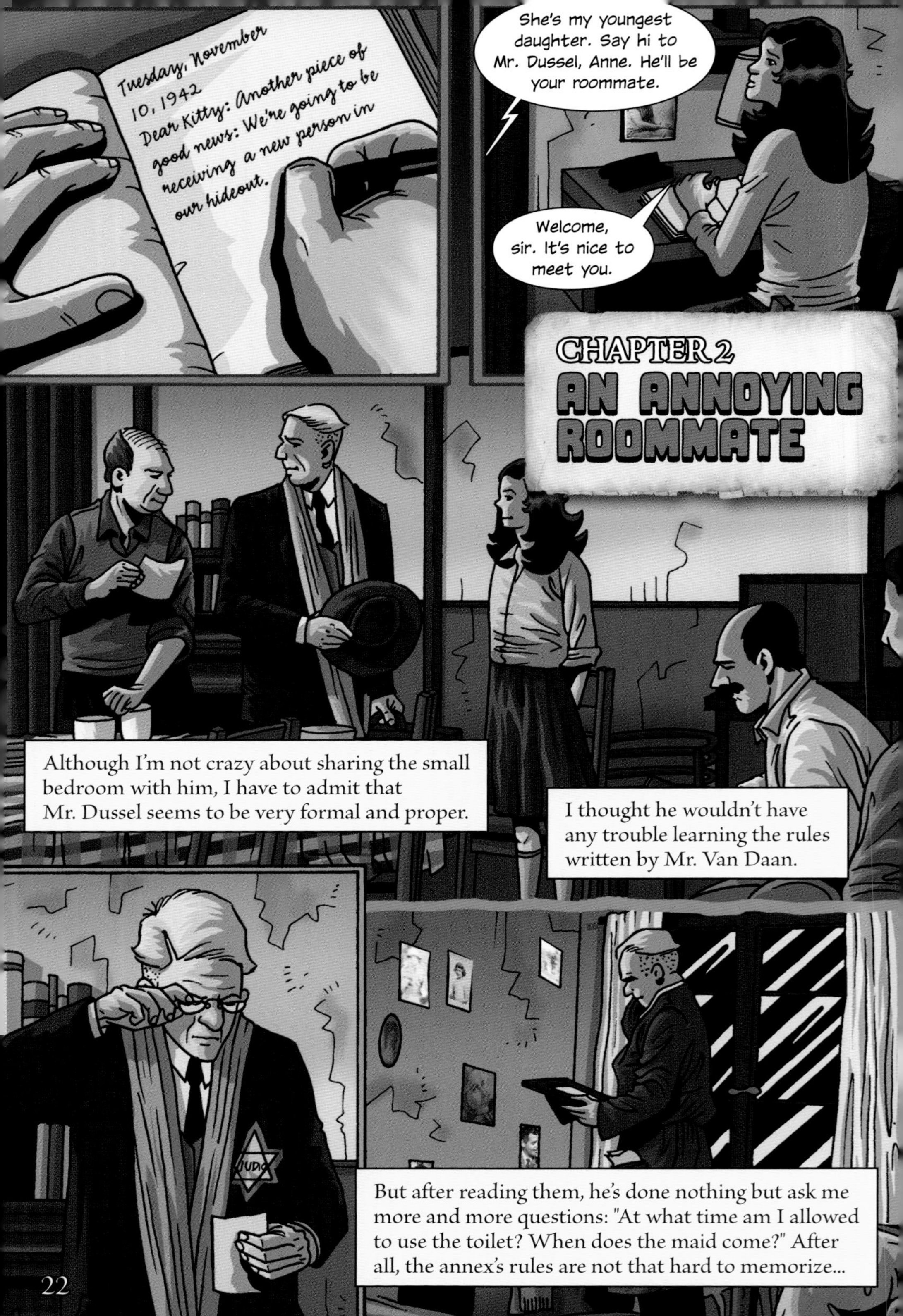
Tuesday, November 10, 1942
Dear Kitty: Another piece of good news: We're going to be receiving a new person in our hideout.
She's my youngest daughter. Say hi to Mr. Dussel, Anne. He'll be your roommate.
Welcome, sir. It's nice to meet you.
CHAPTER 2
AN ANNOYING ROOMMATE
Although I'm not crazy about sharing the small bedroom with him, I have to admit that Mr. Dussel seems to be very formal and proper.
I thought he wouldn't have any trouble learning the rules written by Mr. Van Daan.
JUDE
But after reading them, he's done nothing but ask me more and more questions: "At what time am I allowed to use the toilet? When does the maid come?" After all, the annex's rules are not that hard to memorize...

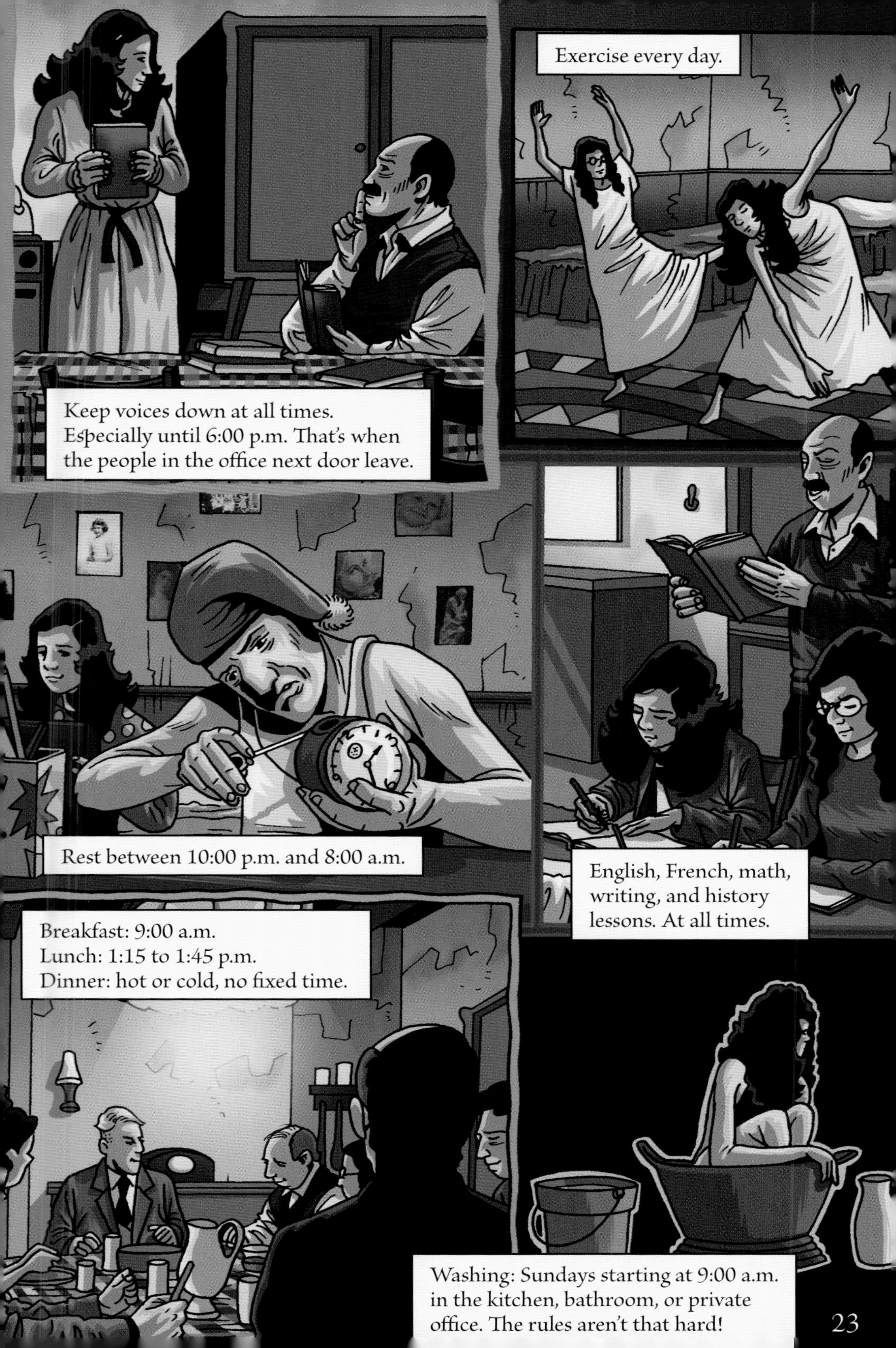
Keep voices down at all times. Especially until 6:00 p.m. That's when the people in the office next door leave.
Exercise every day.
Rest between 10:00 p.m. and 8:00 a.m.
English, French, math, writing, and history lessons. At all times.
Breakfast: 9:00 a.m.
Lunch: 1:15 to 1:45 p.m.
Dinner: hot or cold, no fixed time.
Washing: Sundays starting at 9:00 a.m. in the kitchen, bathroom, or private office. The rules aren't that hard!

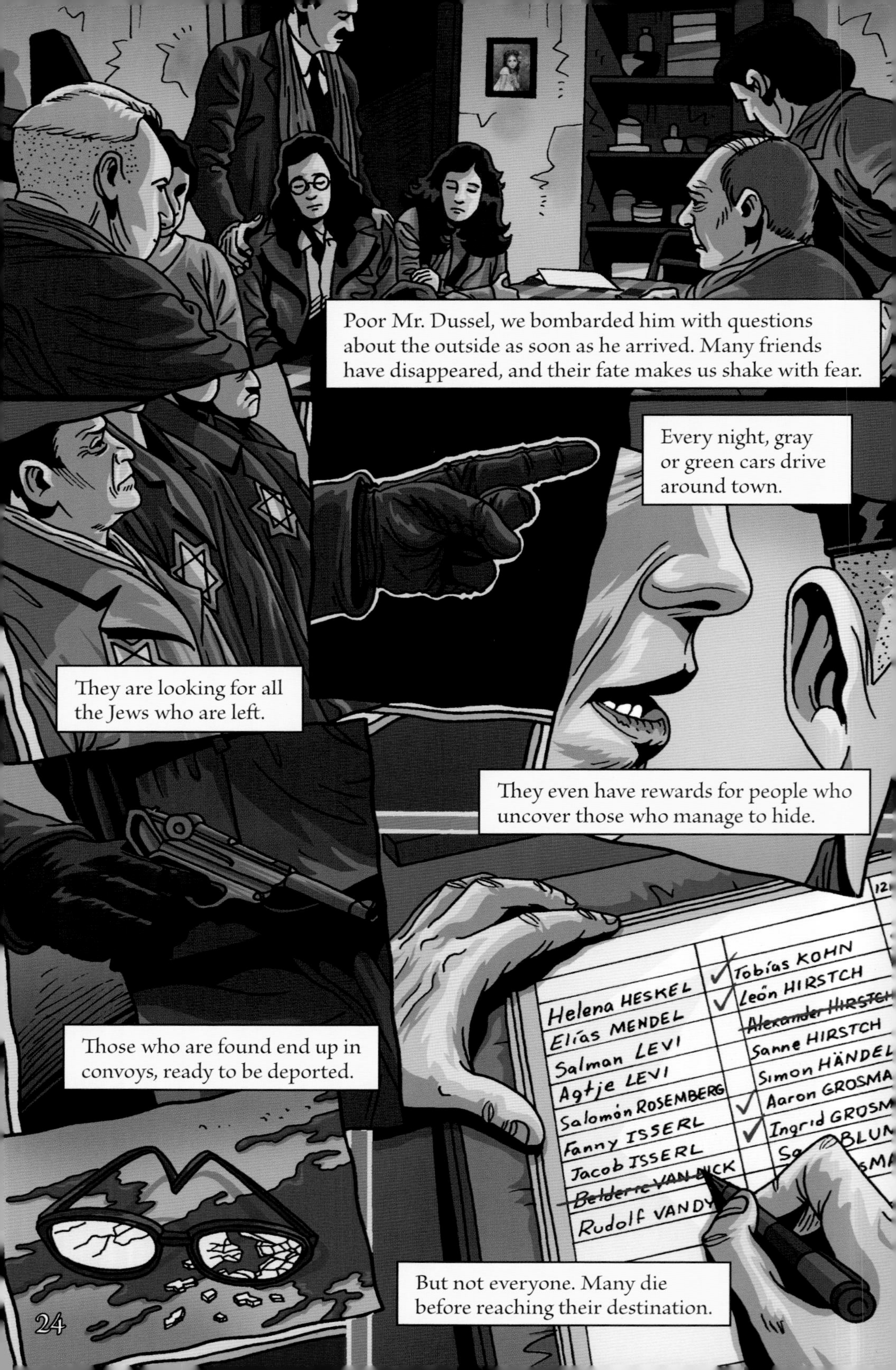
Poor Mr. Dussel, we bombarded him with questions about the outside as soon as he arrived. Many friends have disappeared, and their fate makes us shake with fear.
Every night, gray or green cars drive around town.
They are looking for all the Jews who are left.
They even have rewards for people who uncover those who manage to hide.
Those who are found end up in convoys, ready to be deported.
Helena HESKEL
Elías MENDEL
Salman LEVI
Agtje LEVI
Salomón ROSEMBERG
Fanny ISSERL
Jacob ISSERL
Rudolf VANDY
Tobías KOHN
León HIRSTCH
Alexander HIRSTCH
Sanne HIRSTCH
Simon HÄNDEL
But not everyone. Many die before reaching their destination.

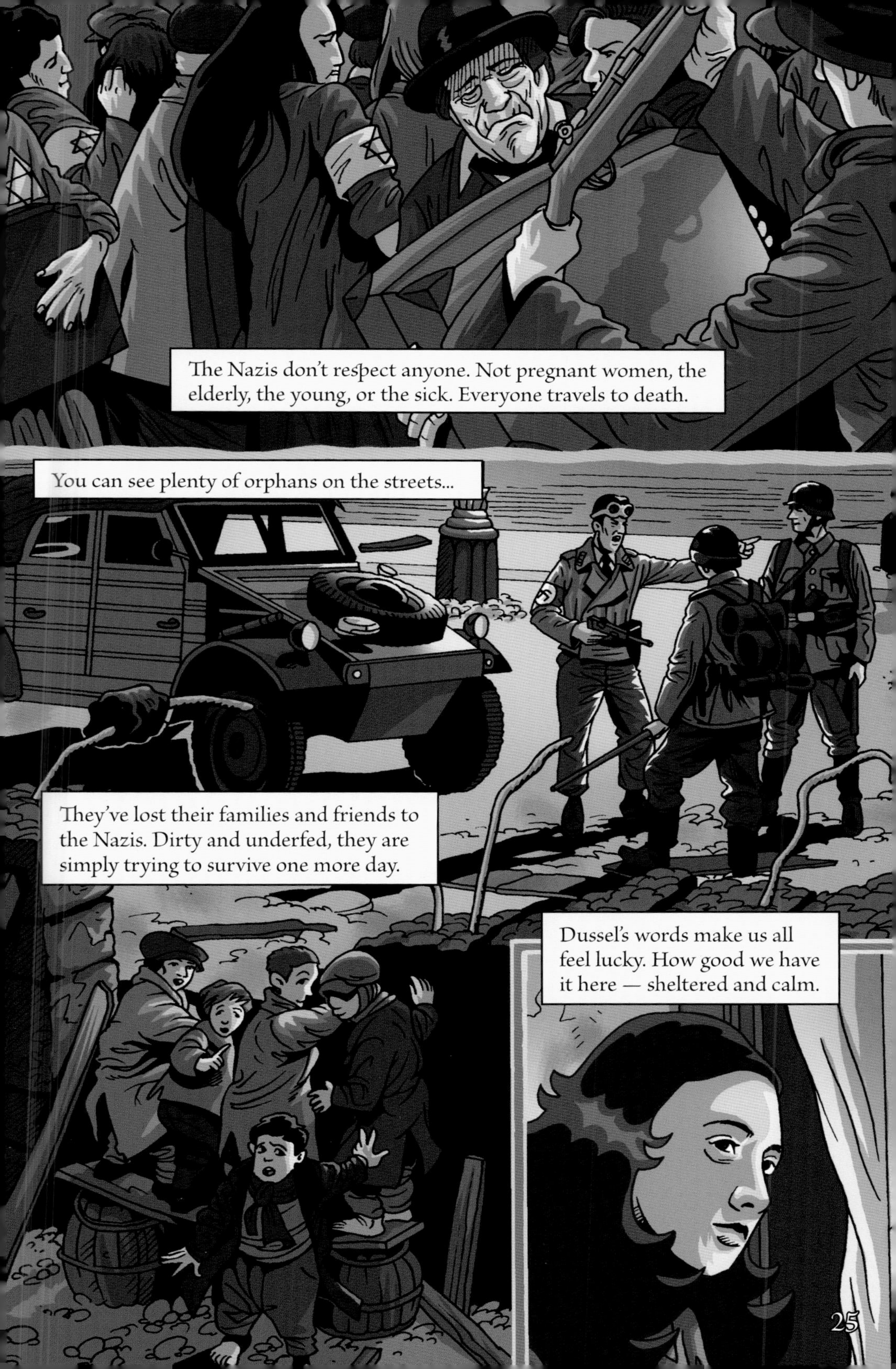
The Nazis don't respect anyone. Not pregnant women, the elderly, the young, or the sick. Everyone travels to death.
You can see plenty of orphans on the streets...
They've lost their families and friends to the Nazis. Dirty and underfed, they are simply trying to survive one more day.
Dussel's words make us all feel lucky. How good we have it here — sheltered and calm.

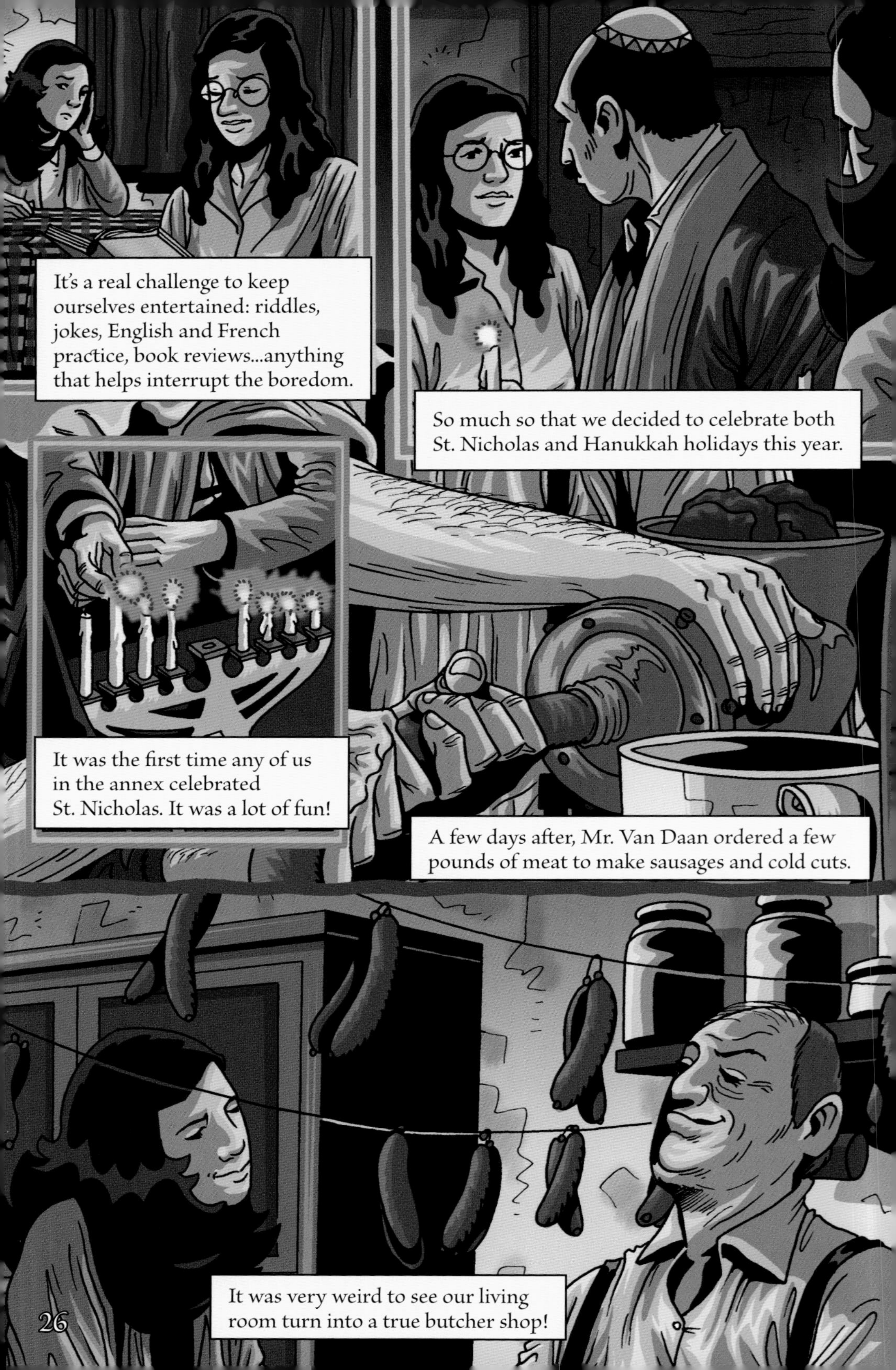
It's a real challenge to keep ourselves entertained: riddles, jokes, English and French practice, book reviews...anything that helps interrupt the boredom.
So much so that we decided to celebrate both St. Nicholas and Hanukkah holidays this year.
It was the first time any of us in the annex celebrated St. Nicholas. It was a lot of fun!
A few days after, Mr. Van Daan ordered a few pounds of meat to make sausages and cold cuts.
It was very weird to see our living room turn into a true butcher shop!

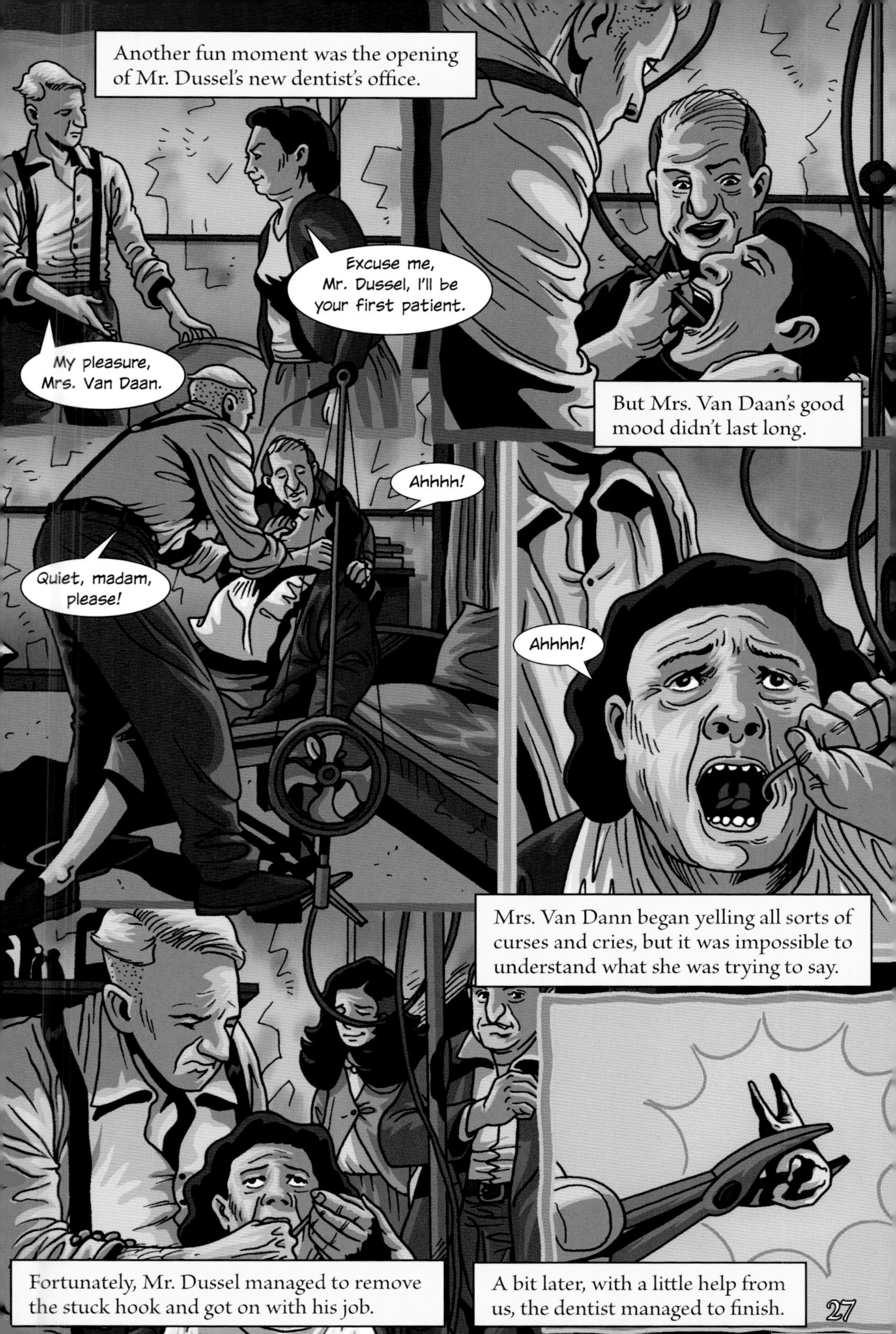

Another fun moment was the opening of Mr. Dussel's new dentist's office.
Excuse me, Mr. Dussel, I'll be your first patient.
My pleasure, Mrs. Van Daan.
But Mrs. Van Daan's good mood didn't last long.
Ahhhh!
Quiet, madam, please!
Ahhhh!
Mrs. Van Dann began yelling all sorts of curses and cries, but it was impossible to understand what she was trying to say.
Fortunately, Mr. Dussel managed to remove the stuck hook and got on with his job.
A bit later, with a little help from us, the dentist managed to finish.

28

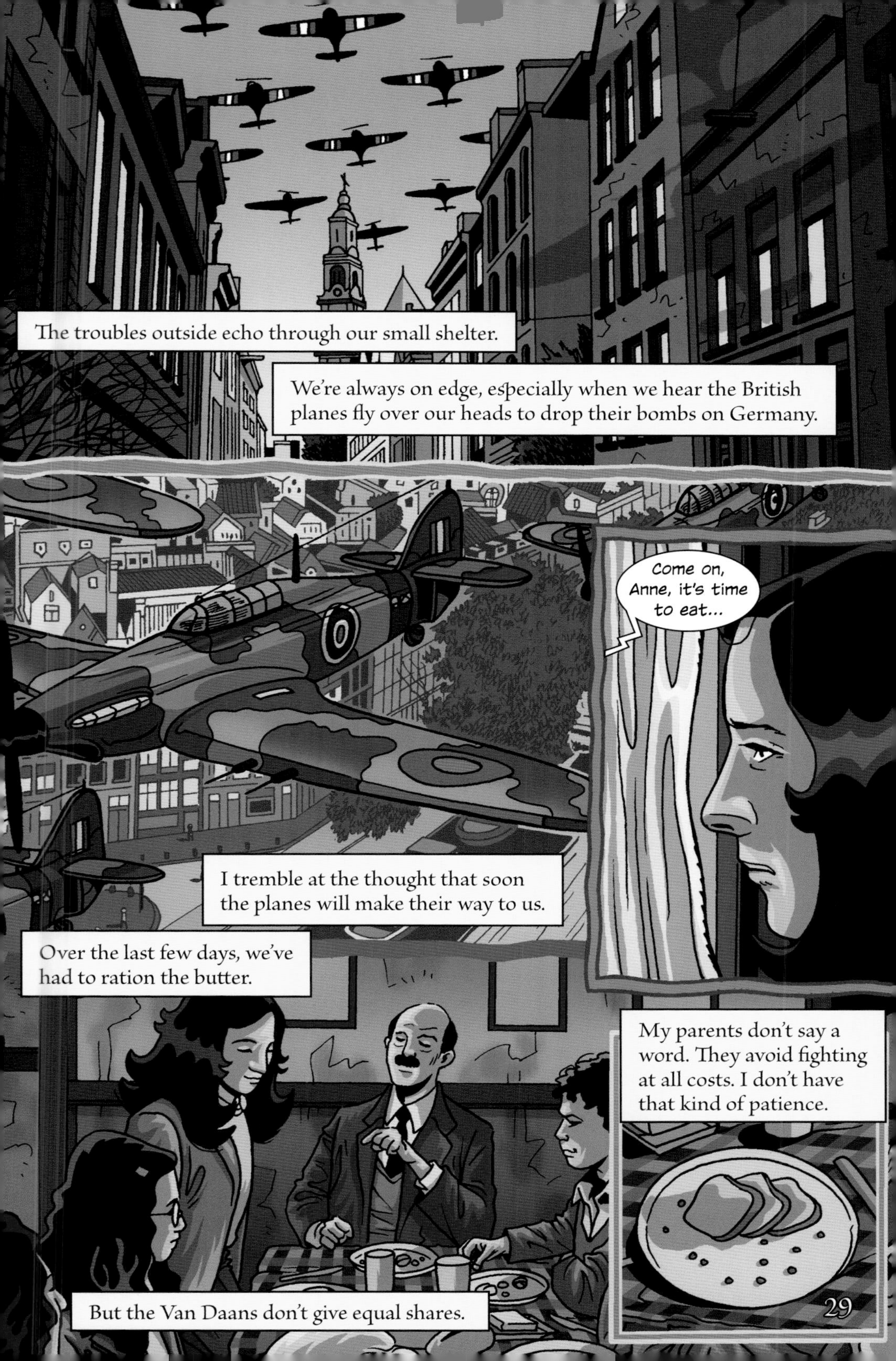
The troubles outside echo through our small shelter.
We're always on edge, especially when we hear the British planes fly over our heads to drop their bombs on Germany.
Come on, Anne, it's time to eat...
I tremble at the thought that soon the planes will make their way to us.
Over the last few days, we've had to ration the butter.
My parents don't say a word. They avoid fighting at all costs. I don't have that kind of patience.
But the Van Daans don't give equal shares.

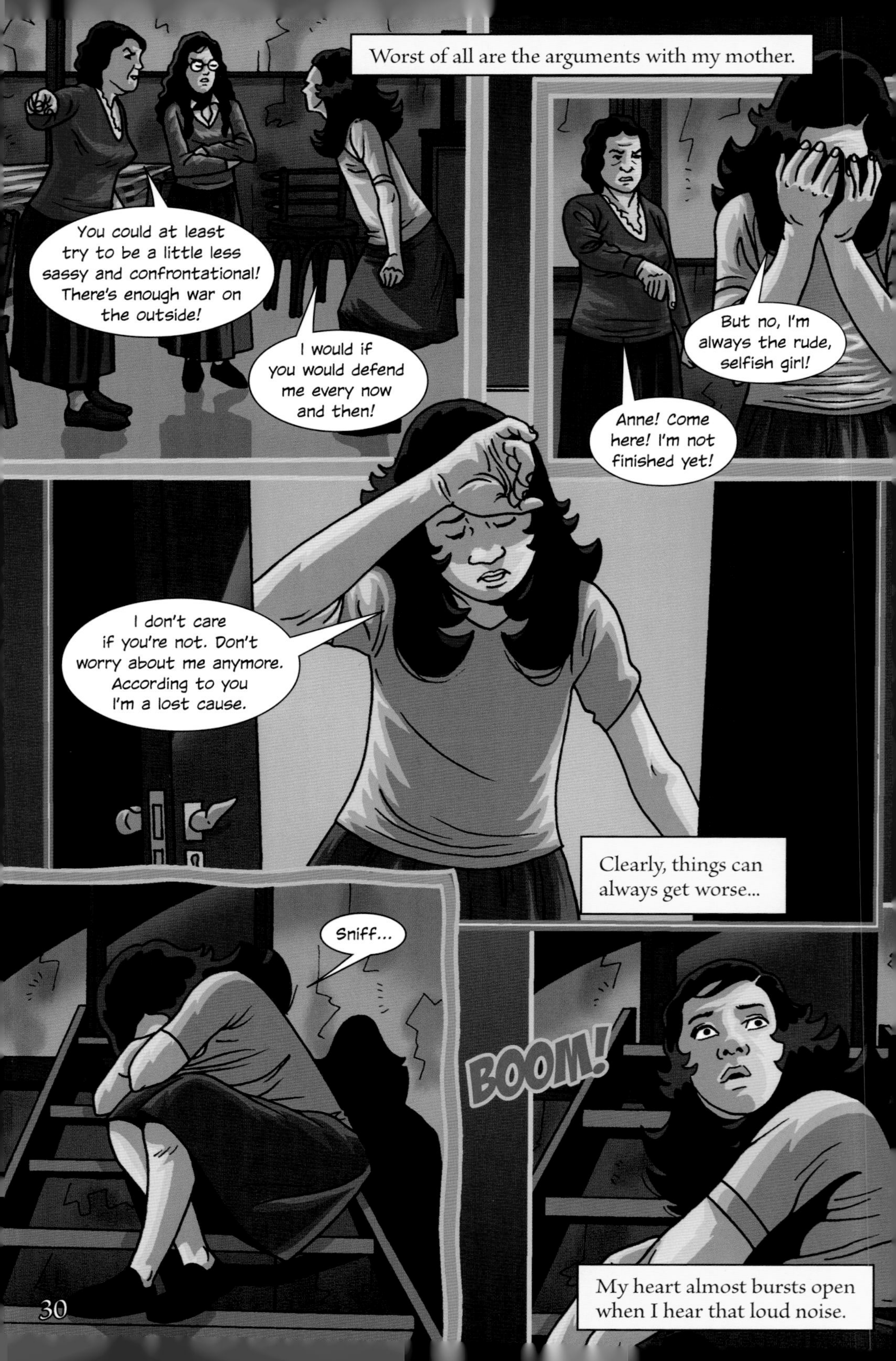
Worst of all are the arguments with my mother.
You could at least try to be a little less sassy and confrontational! There's enough war on the outside!
I would if you would defend me every now and then!
But no, I'm always the rude, selfish girl!
Anne! Come here! I'm not finished yet!
I don't care if you're not. Don't worry about me anymore. According to you I'm a lost cause.
Clearly, things can always get worse...
Sniff...
BOOM!
My heart almost bursts open when I hear that loud noise.

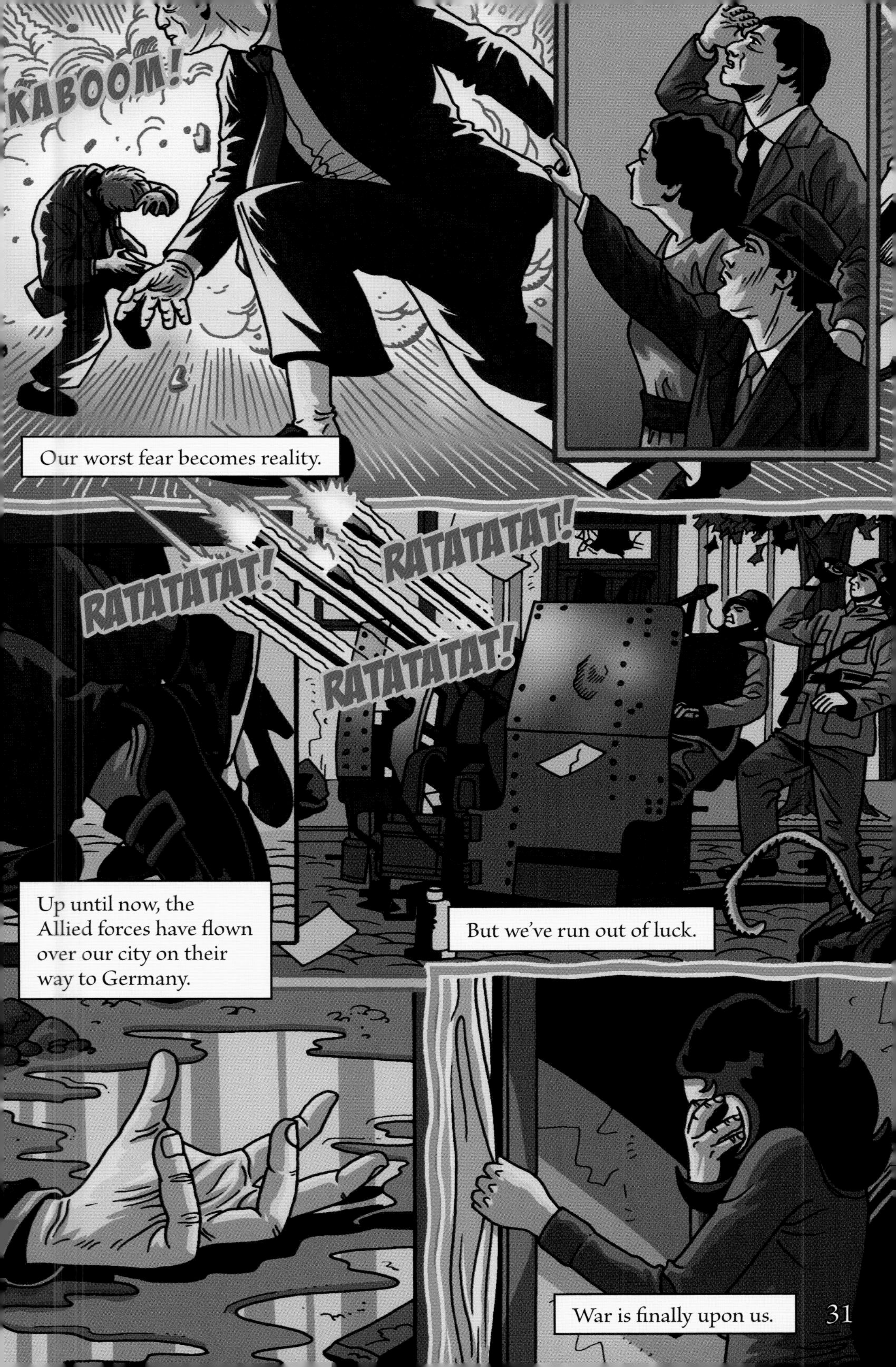
KABOOM!
Our worst fear becomes reality.
RATATATAT!
RATATATAT!
RATATATAT!
Up until now, the Allied forces have flown over our city on their way to Germany.
But we've run out of luck.
War is finally upon us.

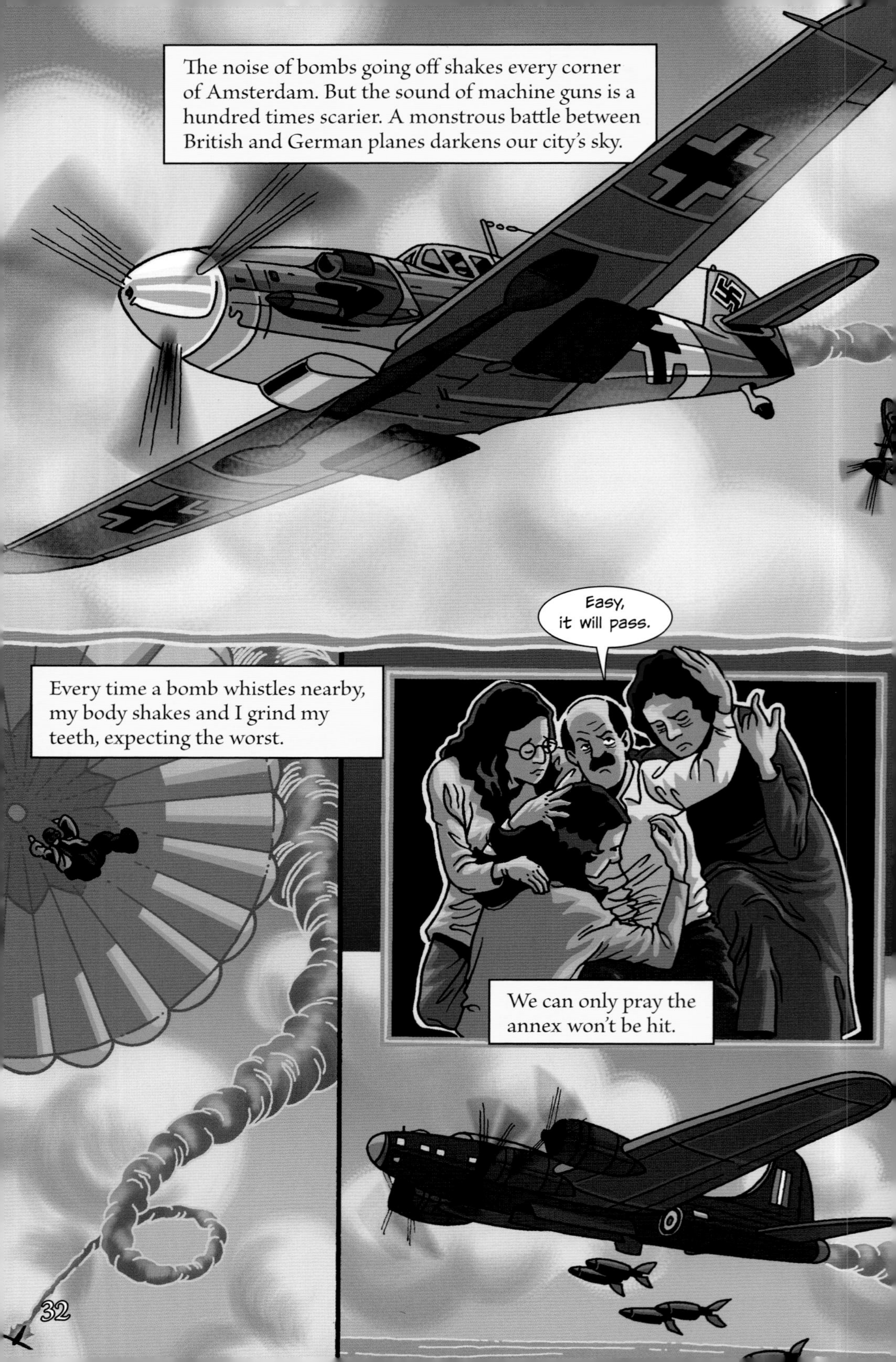
The noise of bombs going off shakes every corner of Amsterdam. But the sound of machine guns is a hundred times scarier. A monstrous battle between British and German planes darkens our city's sky.
Every time a bomb whistles nearby, my body shakes and I grind my teeth, expecting the worst.
Easy, it will pass.
We can only pray the annex won't be hit.

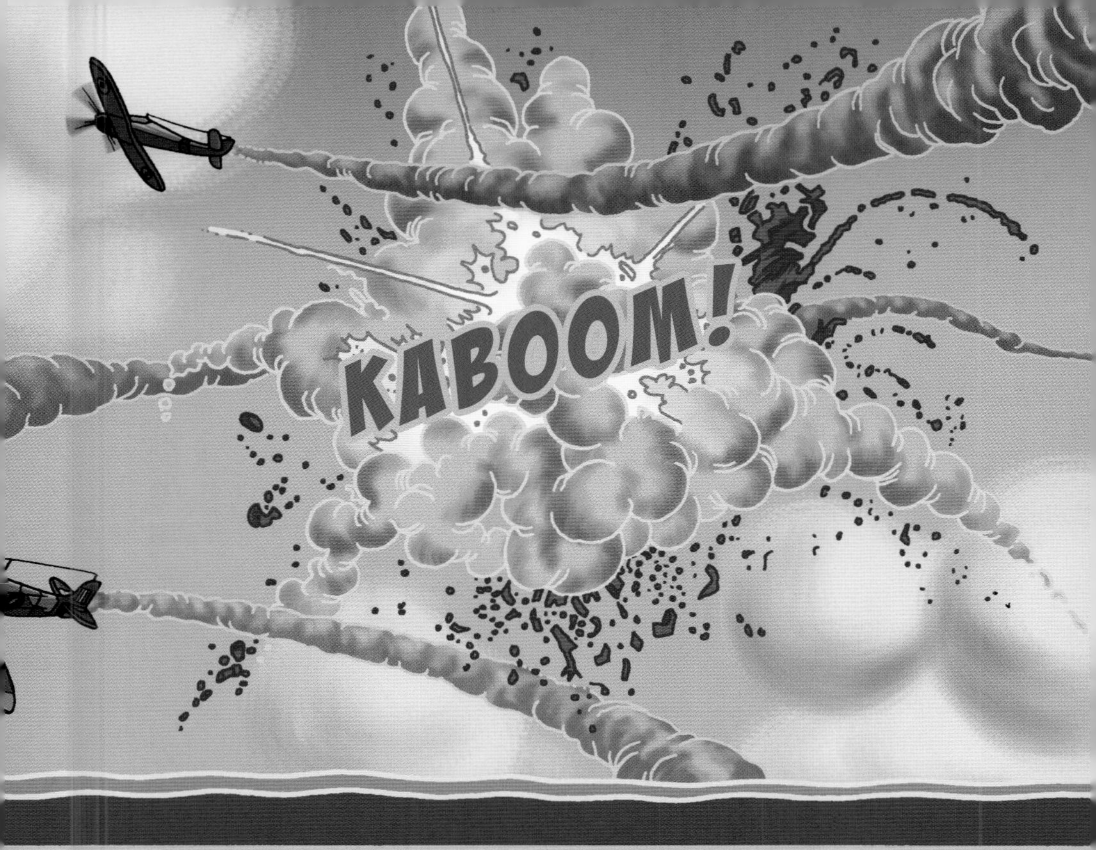
KABOOM!

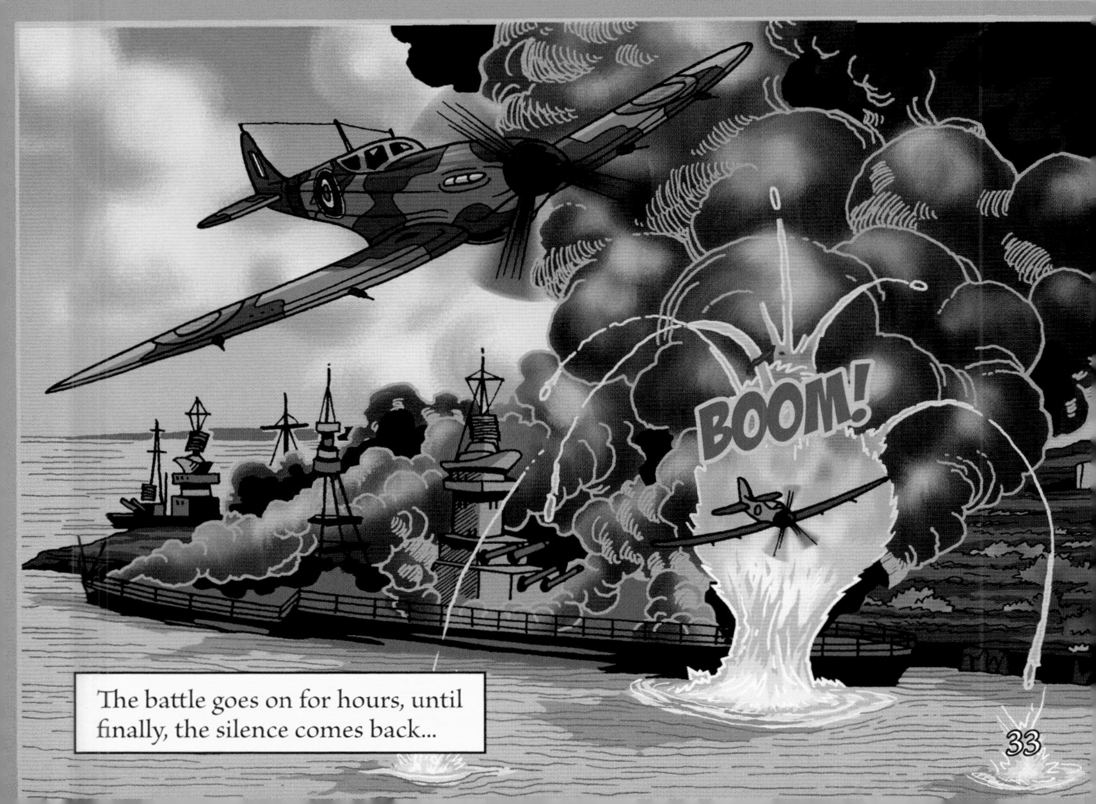
BOOM!
The battle goes on for hours, until finally, the silence comes back...

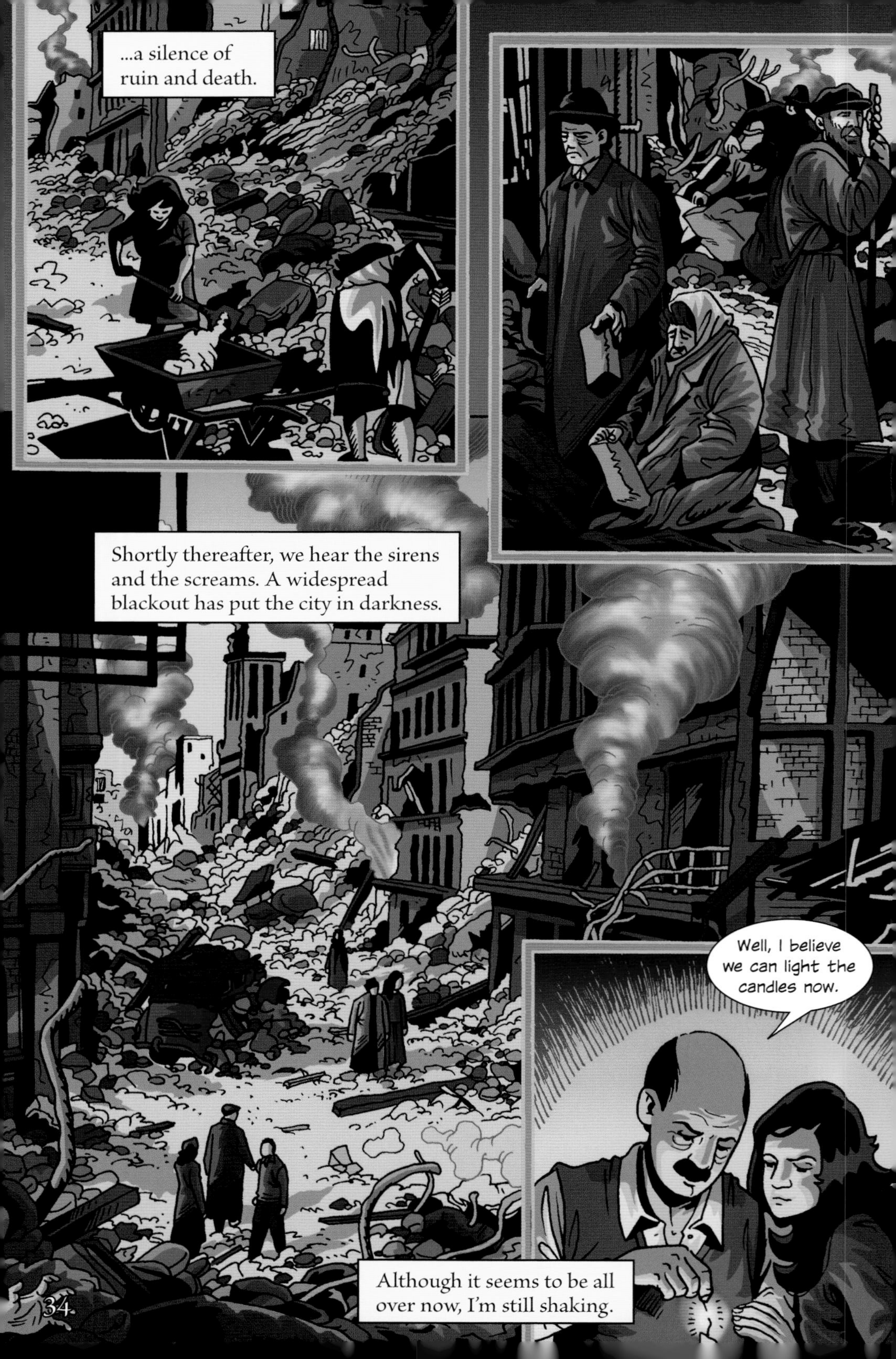
...a silence of ruin and death.
Shortly thereafter, we hear the sirens and the screams. A widespread blackout has put the city in darkness.
Well, I believe we can light the candles now.
Although it seems to be all over now, I'm still shaking.

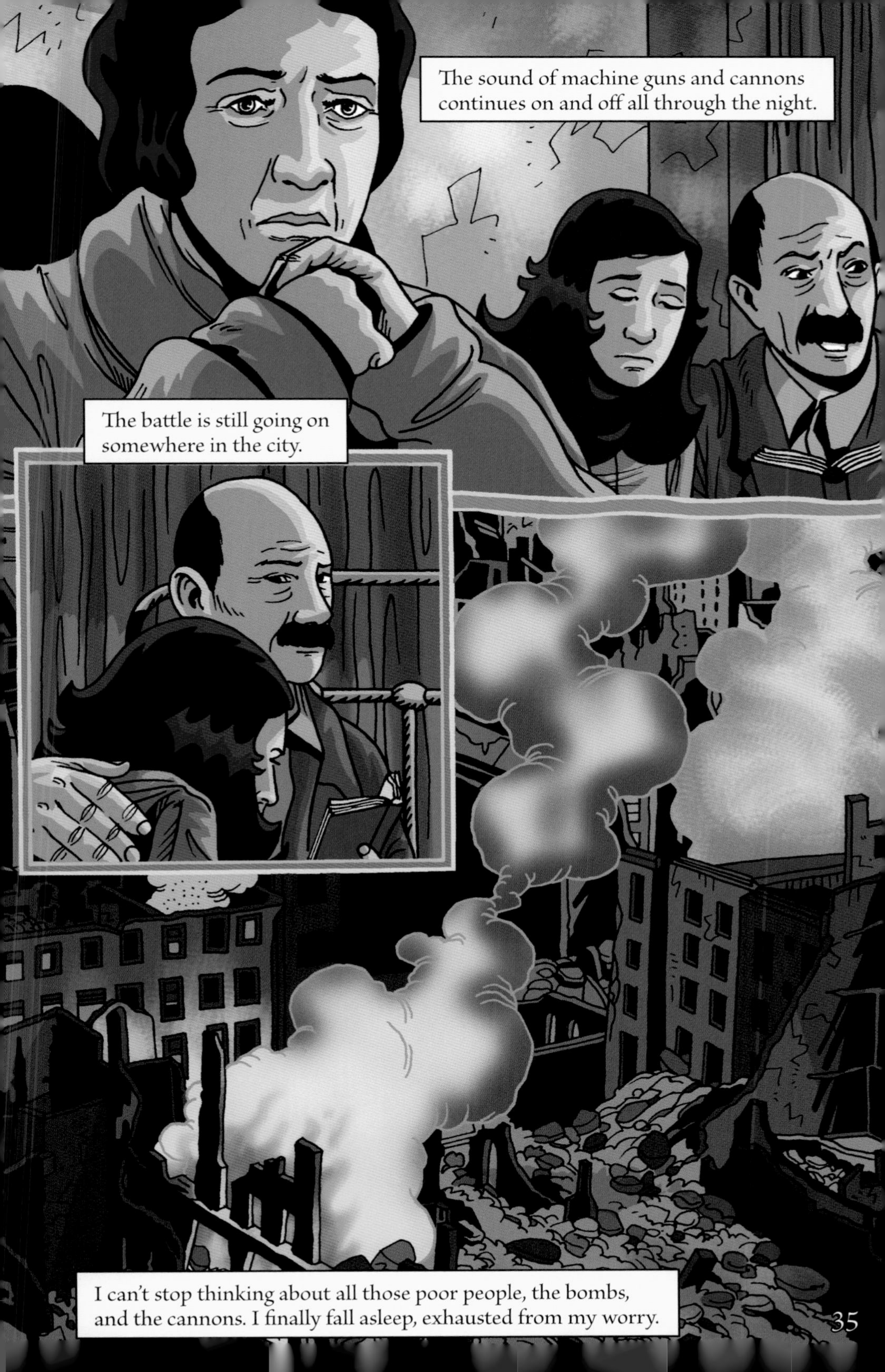
The sound of machine guns and cannons continues on and off all through the night.
The battle is still going on somewhere in the city.
I can't stop thinking about all those poor people, the bombs, and the cannons. I finally fall asleep, exhausted from my worry.

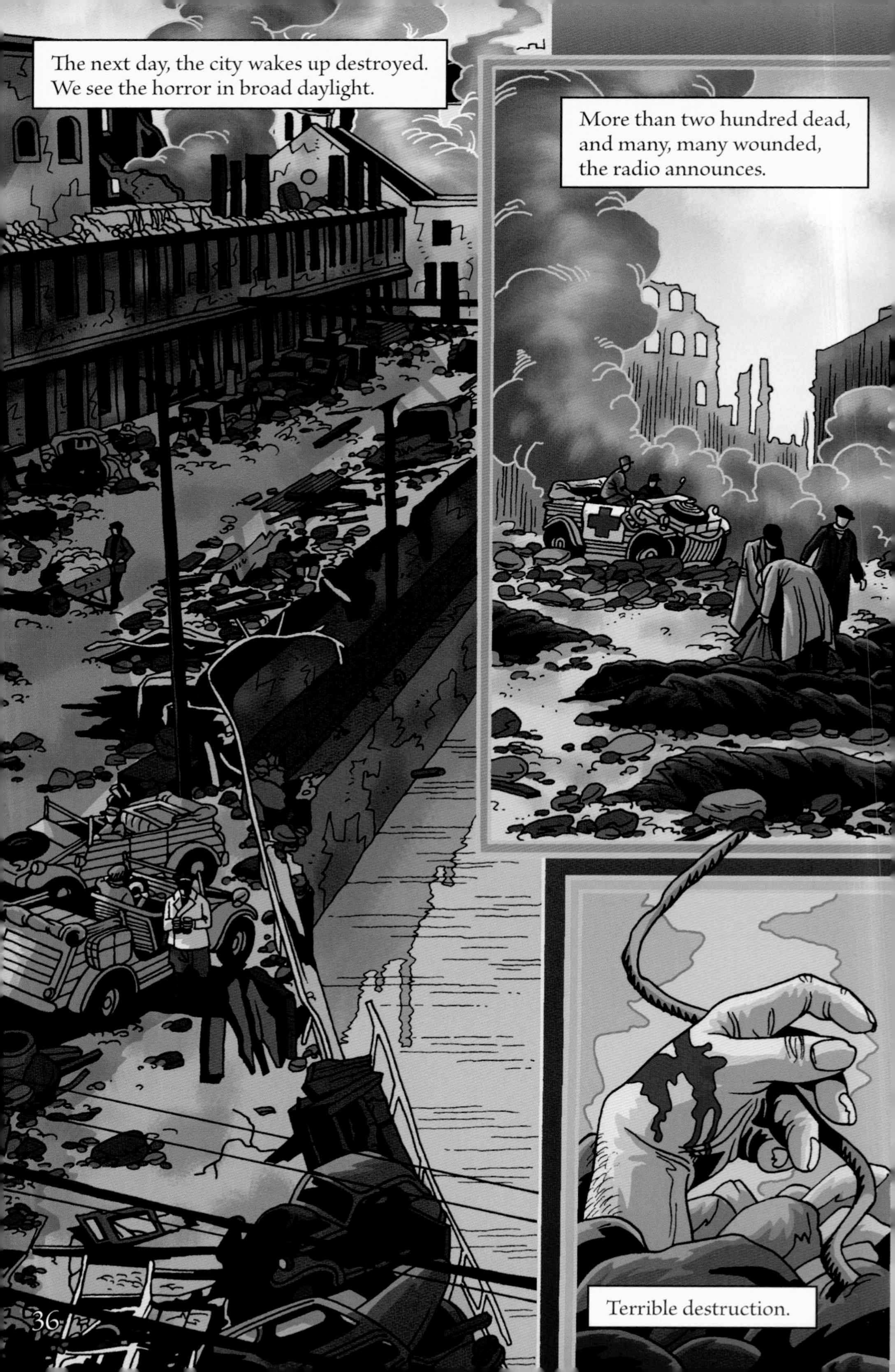
The next day, the city wakes up destroyed. We see the horror in broad daylight.
More than two hundred dead, and many, many wounded, the radio announces.
Terrible destruction.

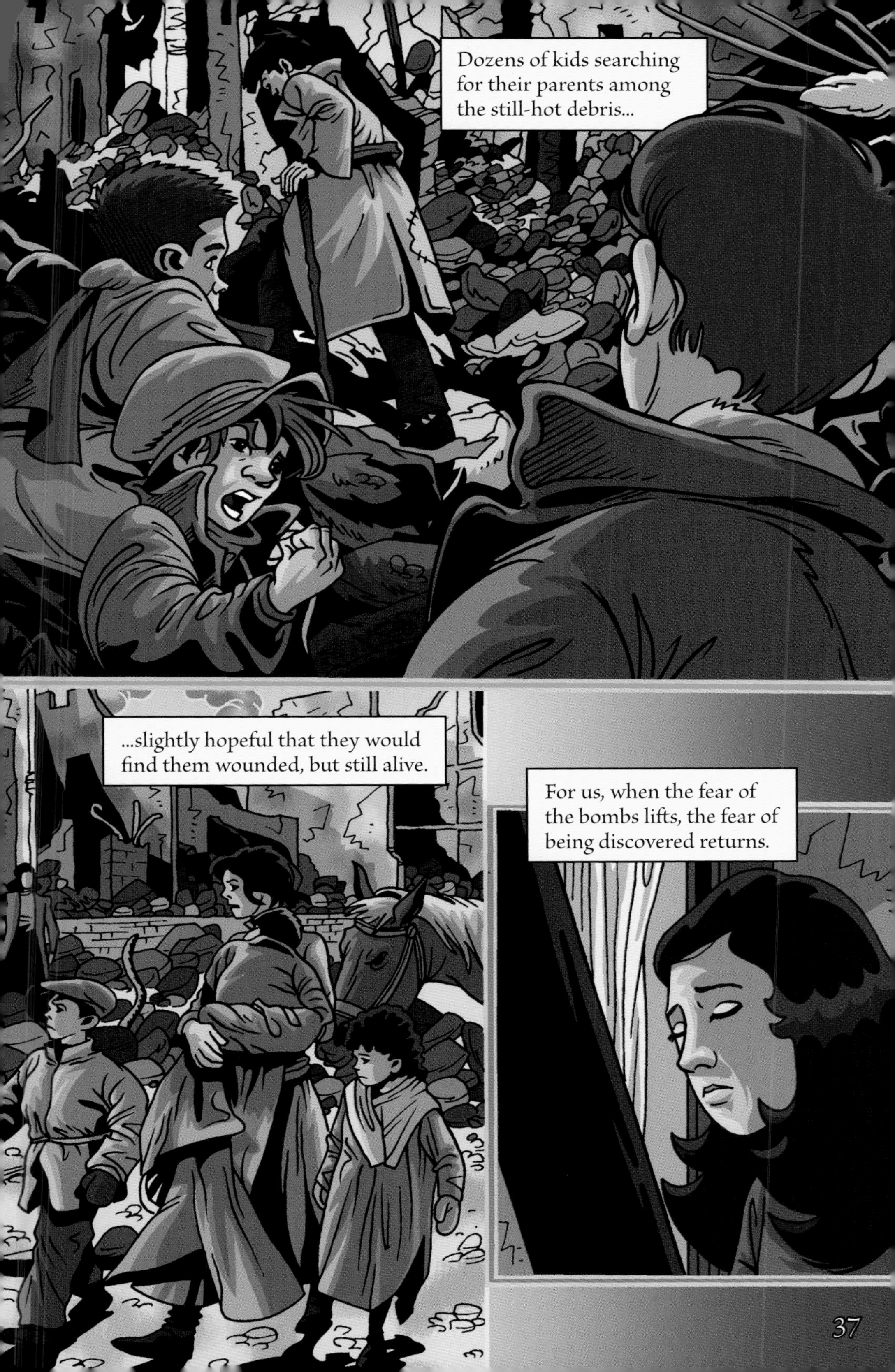
Dozens of kids searching for their parents among the still-hot debris...
...slightly hopeful that they would find them wounded, but still alive.
For us, when the fear of the bombs lifts, the fear of being discovered returns.

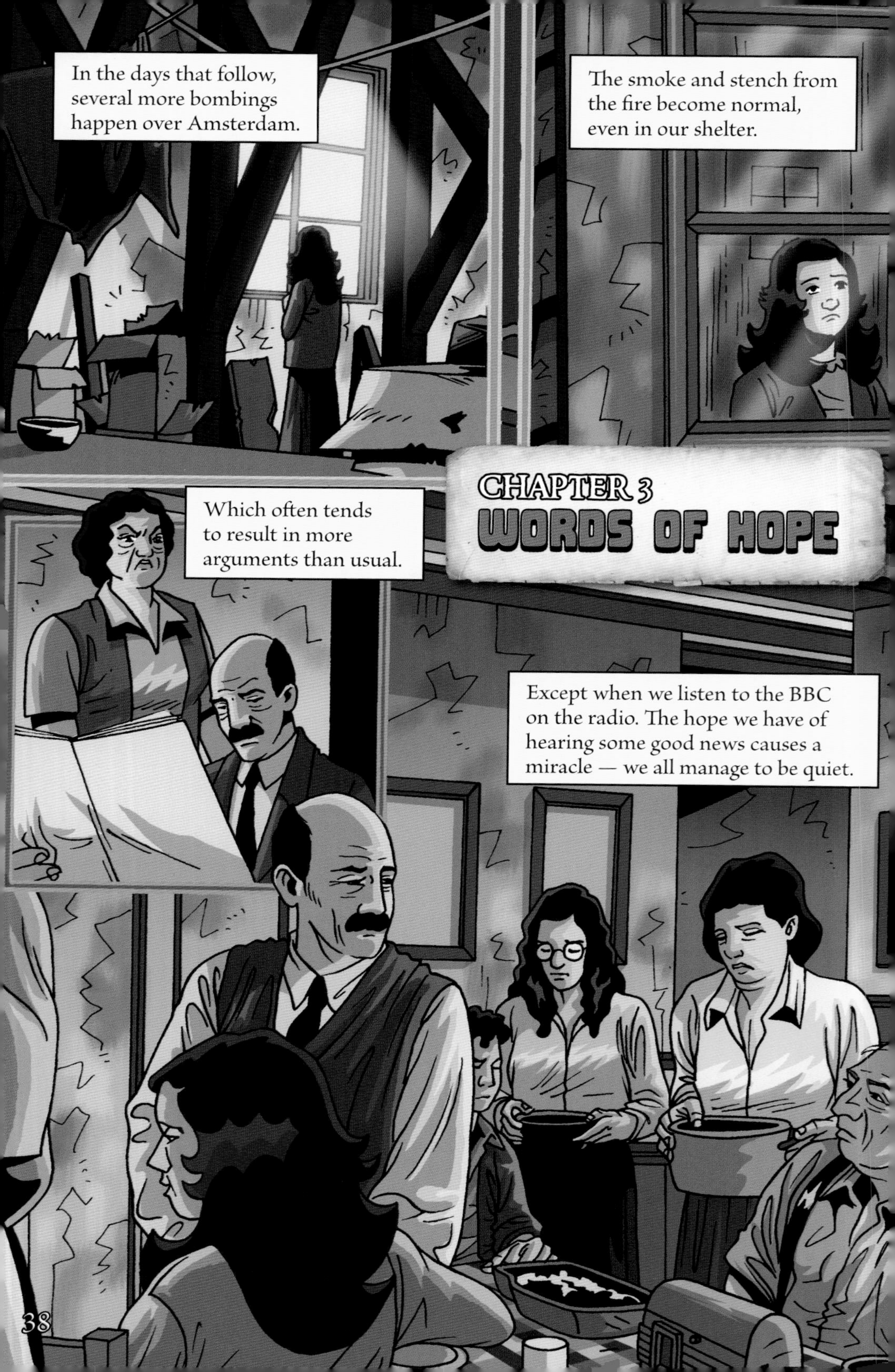
In the days that follow, several more bombings happen over Amsterdam.
The smoke and stench from the fire become normal, even in our shelter.
Which often tends to result in more arguments than usual.
CHAPTER 3
WORDS OF HOPE
Except when we listen to the BBC on the radio. The hope we have of hearing some good news causes a miracle — we all manage to be quiet.

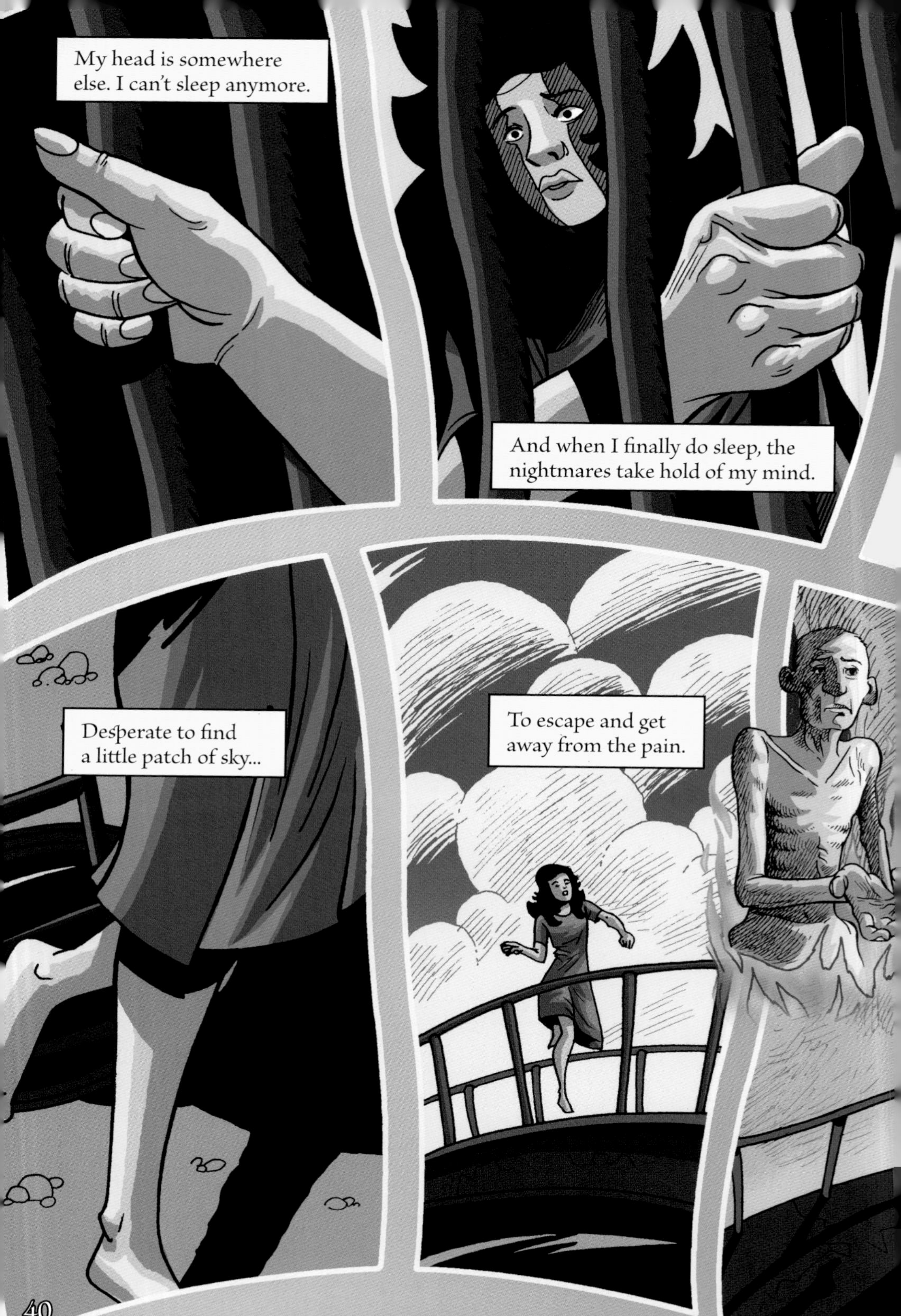
My head is somewhere else. I can't sleep anymore.
And when I finally do sleep, the nightmares take hold of my mind.
Desperate to find a little patch of sky...
To escape and get away from the pain.

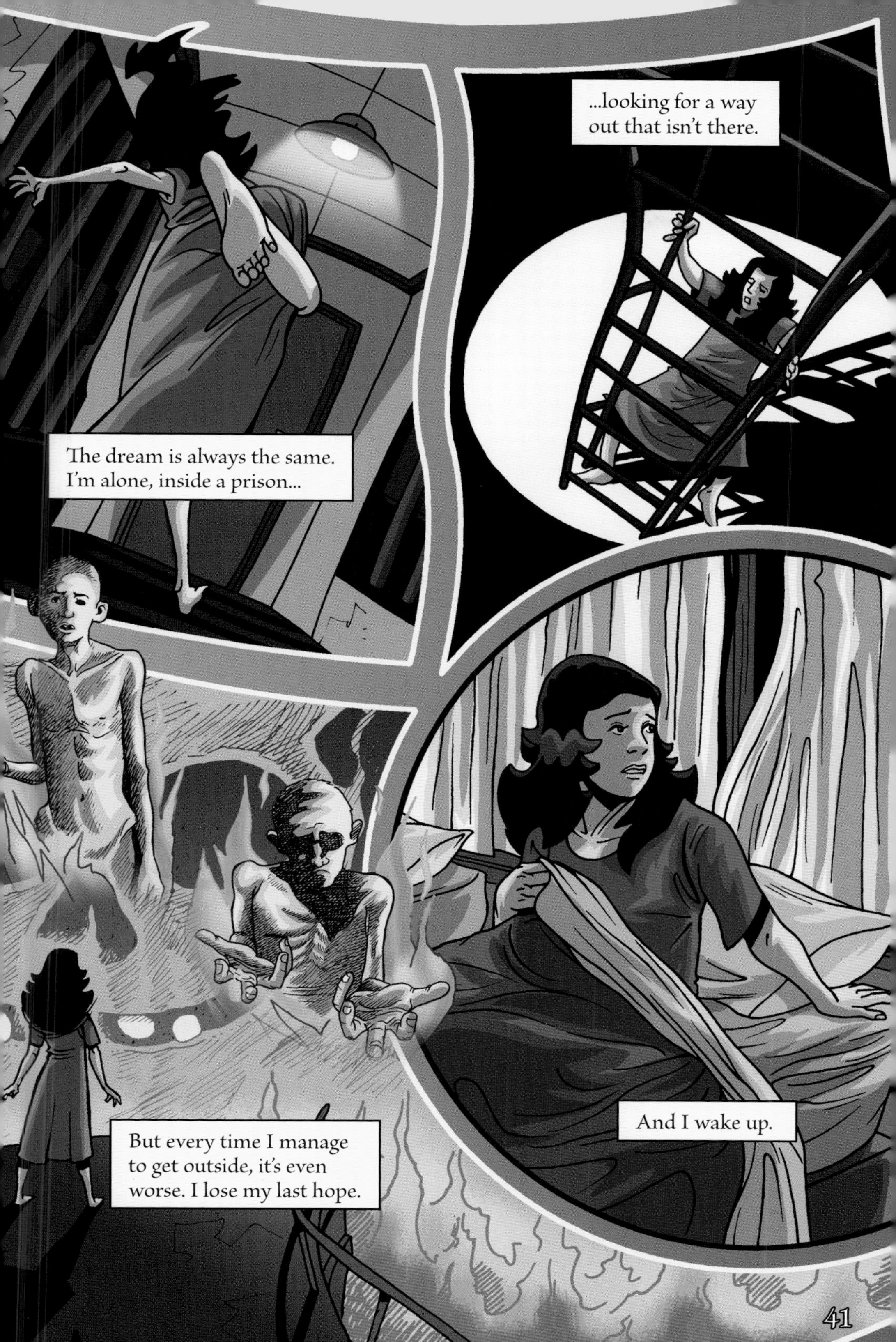
The dream is always the same. I'm alone, inside a prison...
...looking for a way out that isn't there.
But every time I manage to get outside, it's even worse. I lose my last hope.
And I wake up.

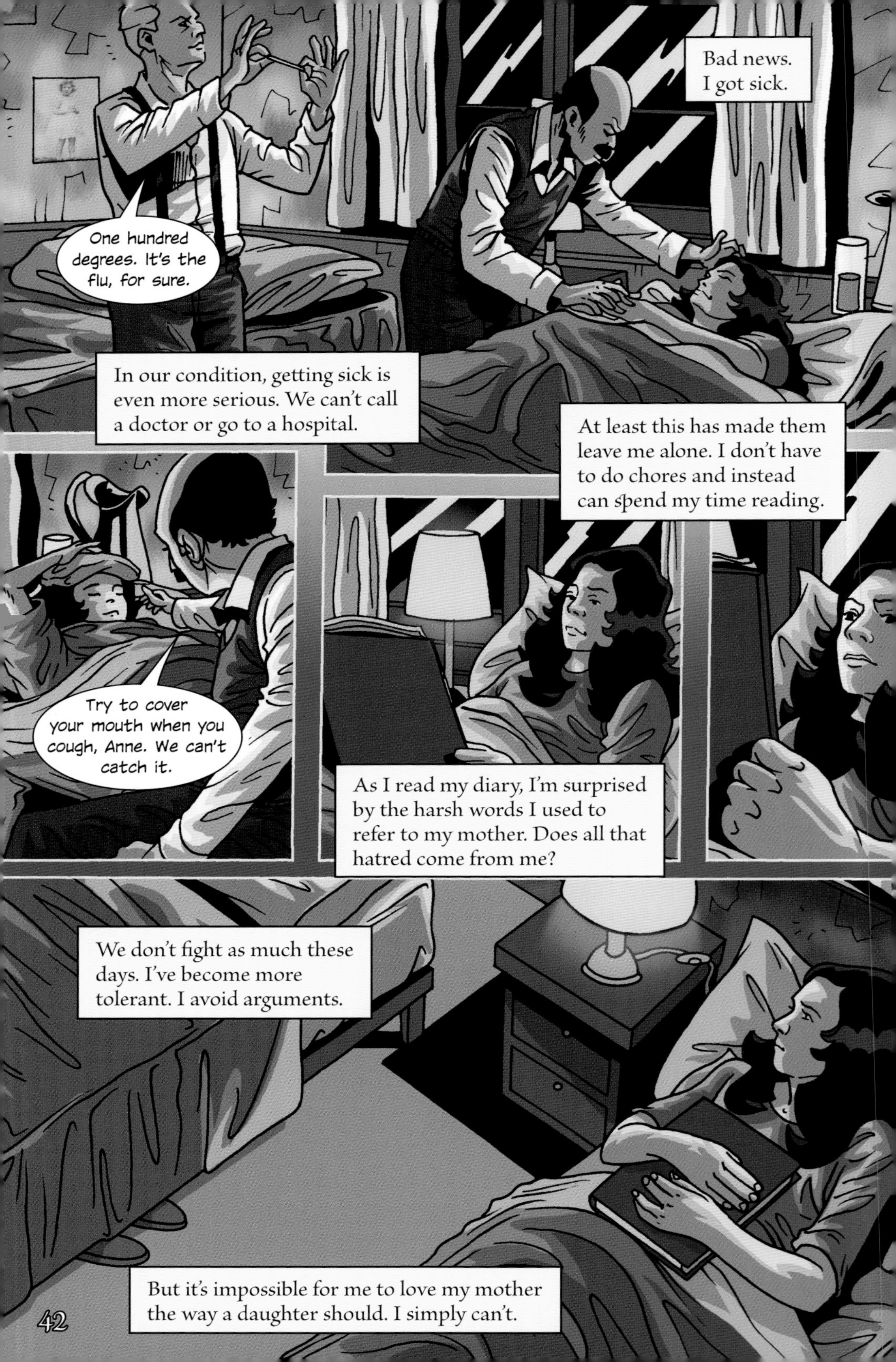
Bad news. I got sick.
One hundred degrees. It's the flu, for sure.
In our condition, getting sick is even more serious. We can't call a doctor or go to a hospital.
At least this has made them leave me alone. I don't have to do chores and instead can spend my time reading.
Try to cover your mouth when you cough, Anne. We can't catch it.
As I read my diary, I'm surprised by the harsh words I used to refer to my mother. Does all that hatred come from me?
We don't fight as much these days. I've become more tolerant. I avoid arguments.
But it's impossible for me to love my mother the way a daughter should. I simply can't.

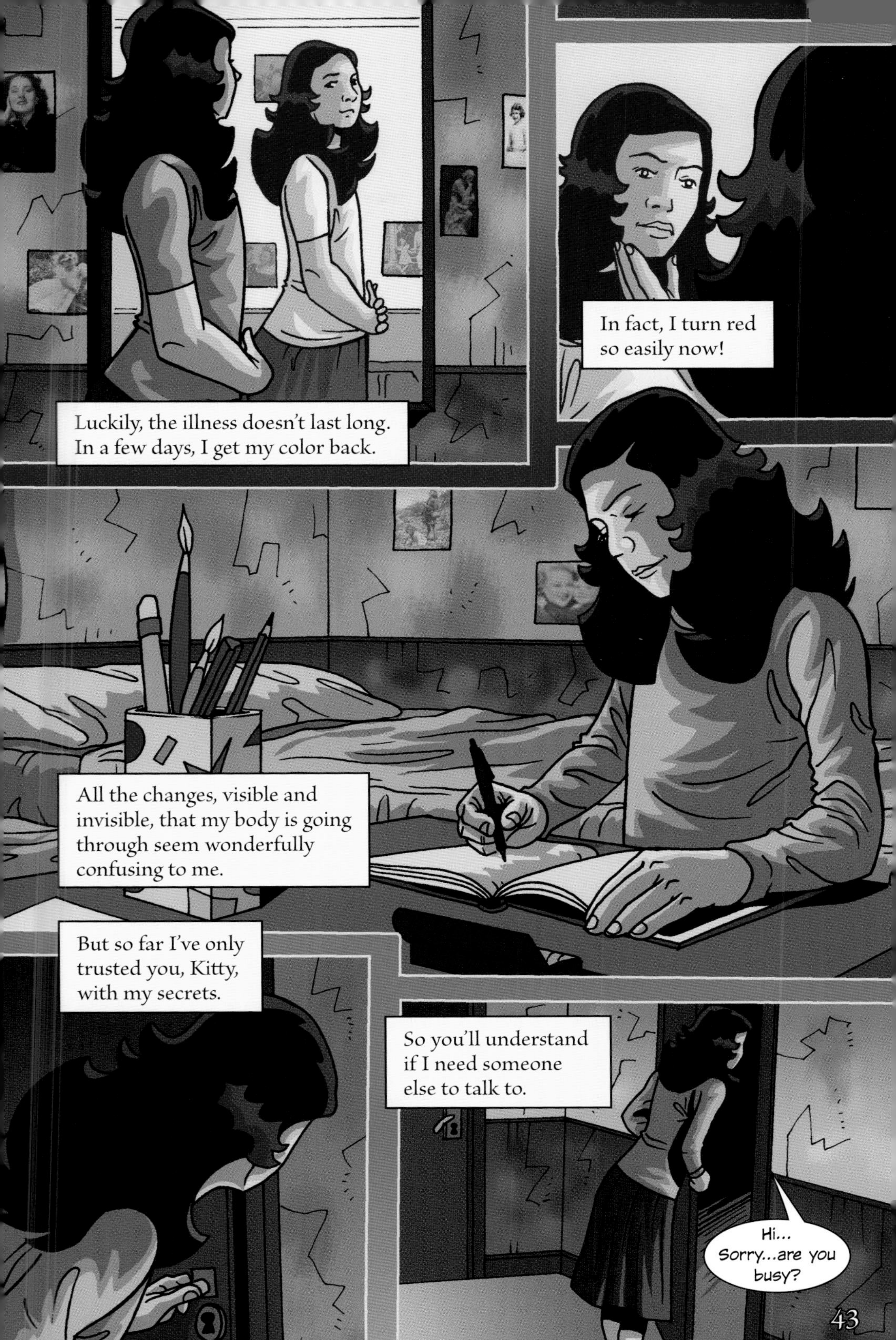
Luckily, the illness doesn't last long. In a few days, I get my color back.
In fact, I turn red so easily now!
All the changes, visible and invisible, that my body is going through seem wonderfully confusing to me.
But so far I've only trusted you, Kitty, with my secrets.
So you'll understand if I need someone else to talk to.
Hi... Sorry...are you busy?

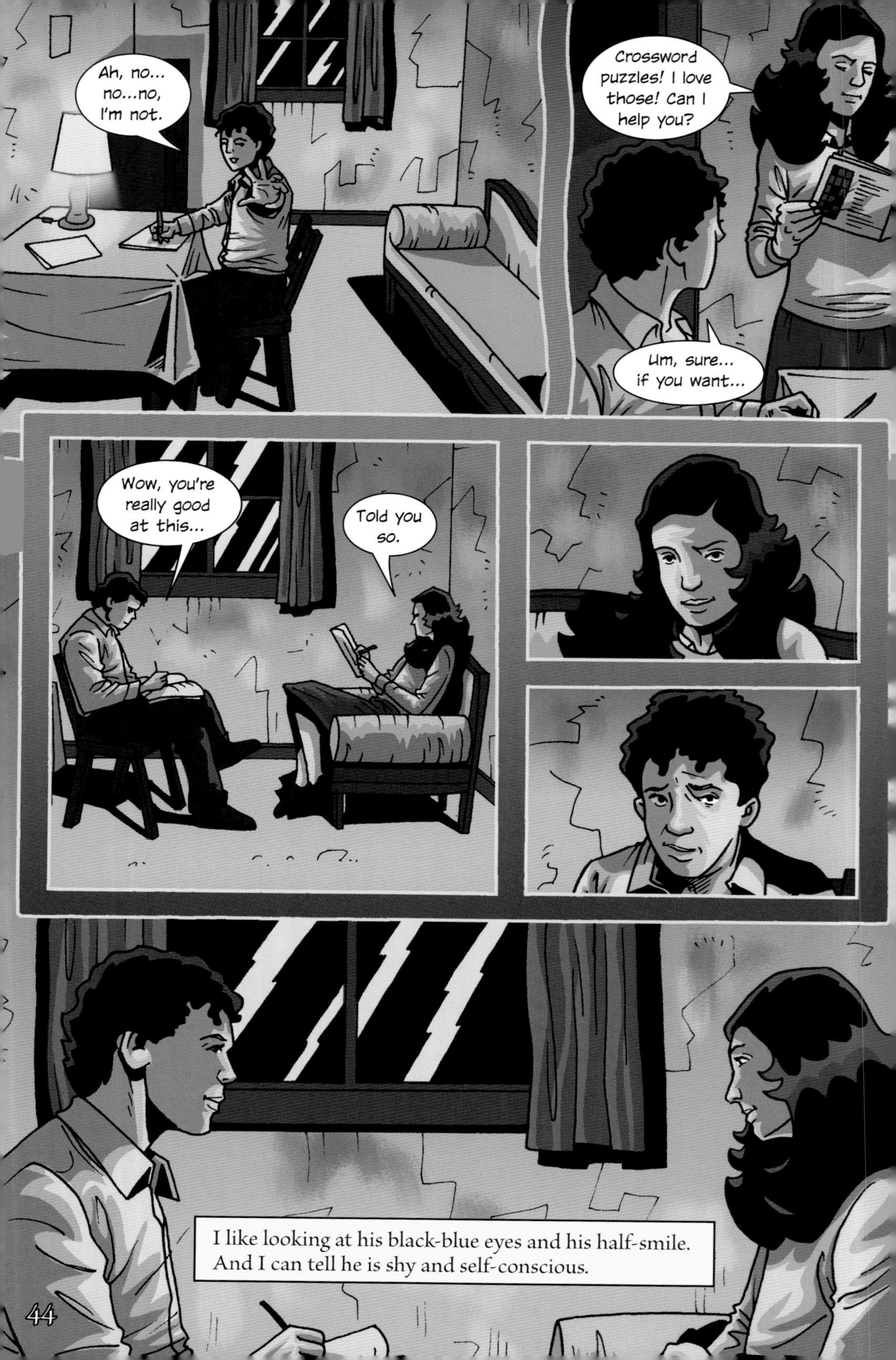

Ah, no...
no...no,
I'm not.
Crossword
puzzles! I love
those! Can I
help you?
Um, sure...
if you want...
Wow, you're
really good
at this...
Told you
so.
I like looking at his black-blue eyes and his half-smile.
And I can tell he is shy and self-conscious.

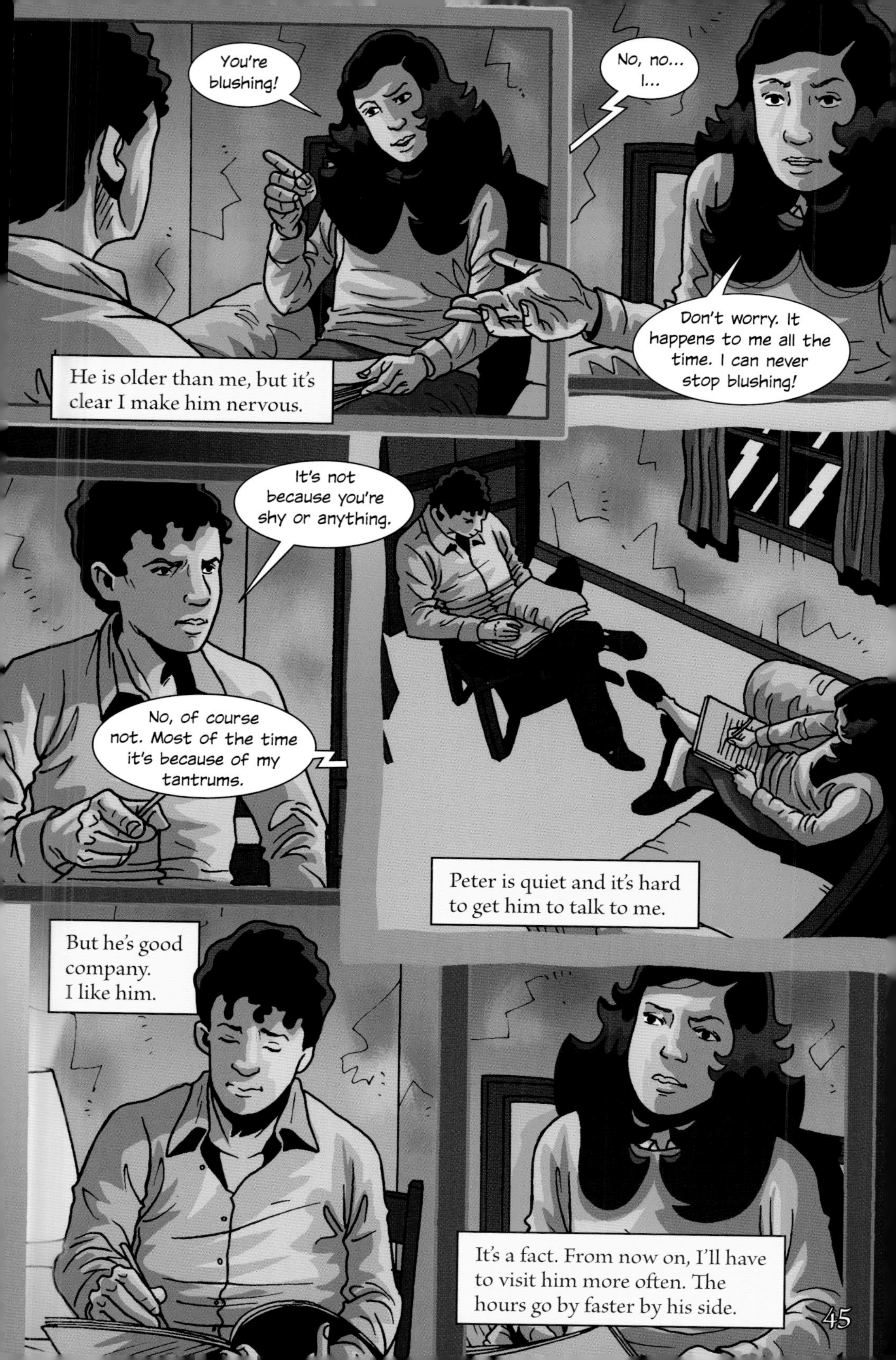
You're blushing!
No, no... I...
He is older than me, but it's clear I make him nervous.
Don't worry. It happens to me all the time. I can never stop blushing!
It's not because you're shy or anything.
No, of course not. Most of the time it's because of my tantrums.
Peter is quiet and it's hard to get him to talk to me.
But he's good company. I like him.
It's a fact. From now on, I'll have to visit him more often. The hours go by faster by his side.

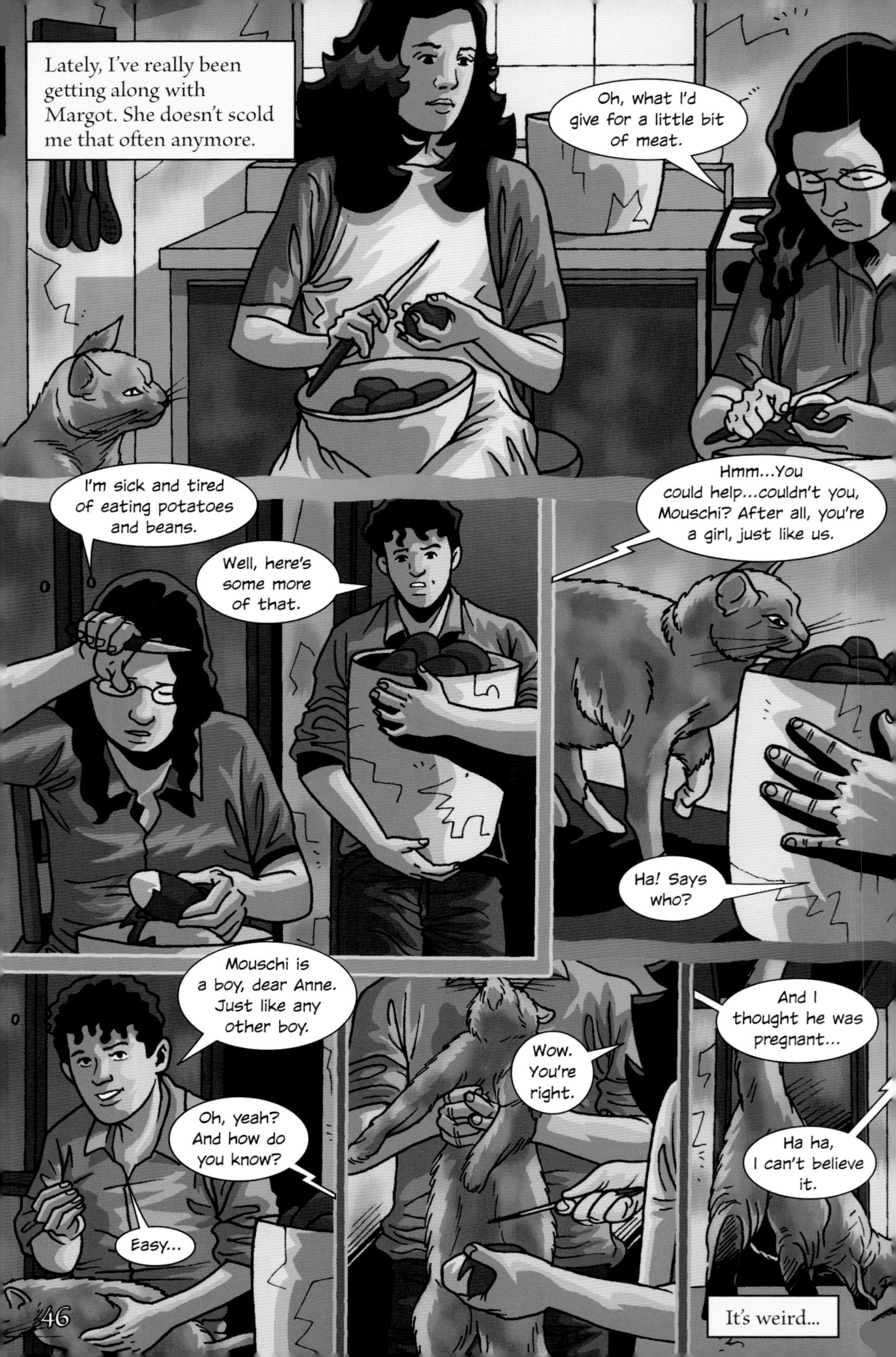

Lately, I've really been getting along with Margot. She doesn't scold me that often anymore.
Oh, what I'd give for a little bit of meat.
I'm sick and tired of eating potatoes and beans.
Well, here's some more of that.
Hmm...You could help...couldn't you, Mouschi? After all, you're a girl, just like us.
Ha! Says who?
Mouschi is a boy, dear Anne. Just like any other boy.
Oh, yeah? And how do you know?
Easy...
Wow. You're right.
And I thought he was pregnant...
Ha ha, I can't believe it.
It's weird...

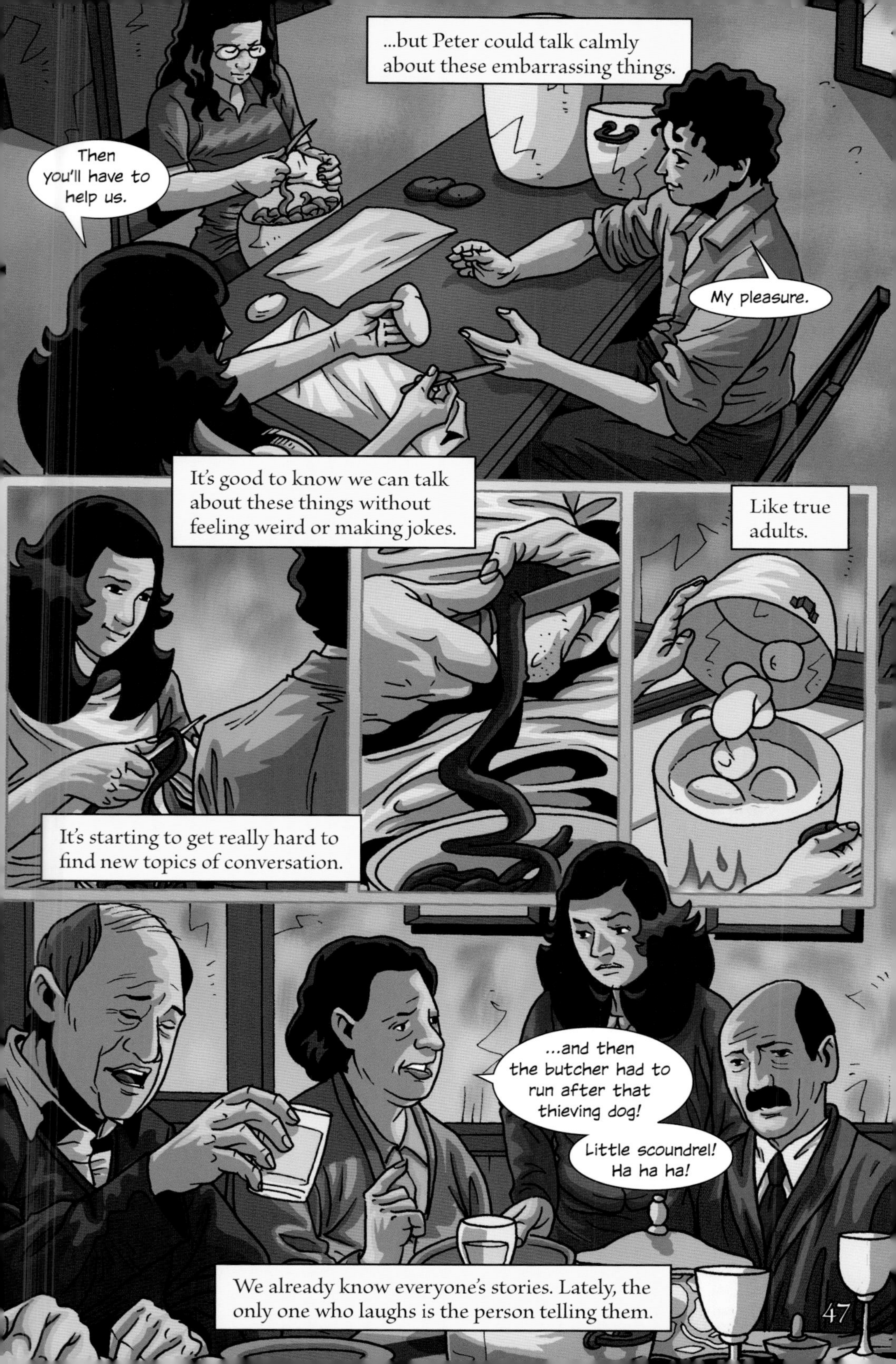

...but Peter could talk calmly about these embarrassing things.
Then you'll have to help us.
My pleasure.
It's good to know we can talk about these things without feeling weird or making jokes.
Like true adults.
It's starting to get really hard to find new topics of conversation.
...and then the butcher had to run after that thieving dog!
Little scoundrel! Ha ha ha!
We already know everyone's stories. Lately, the only one who laughs is the person telling them.

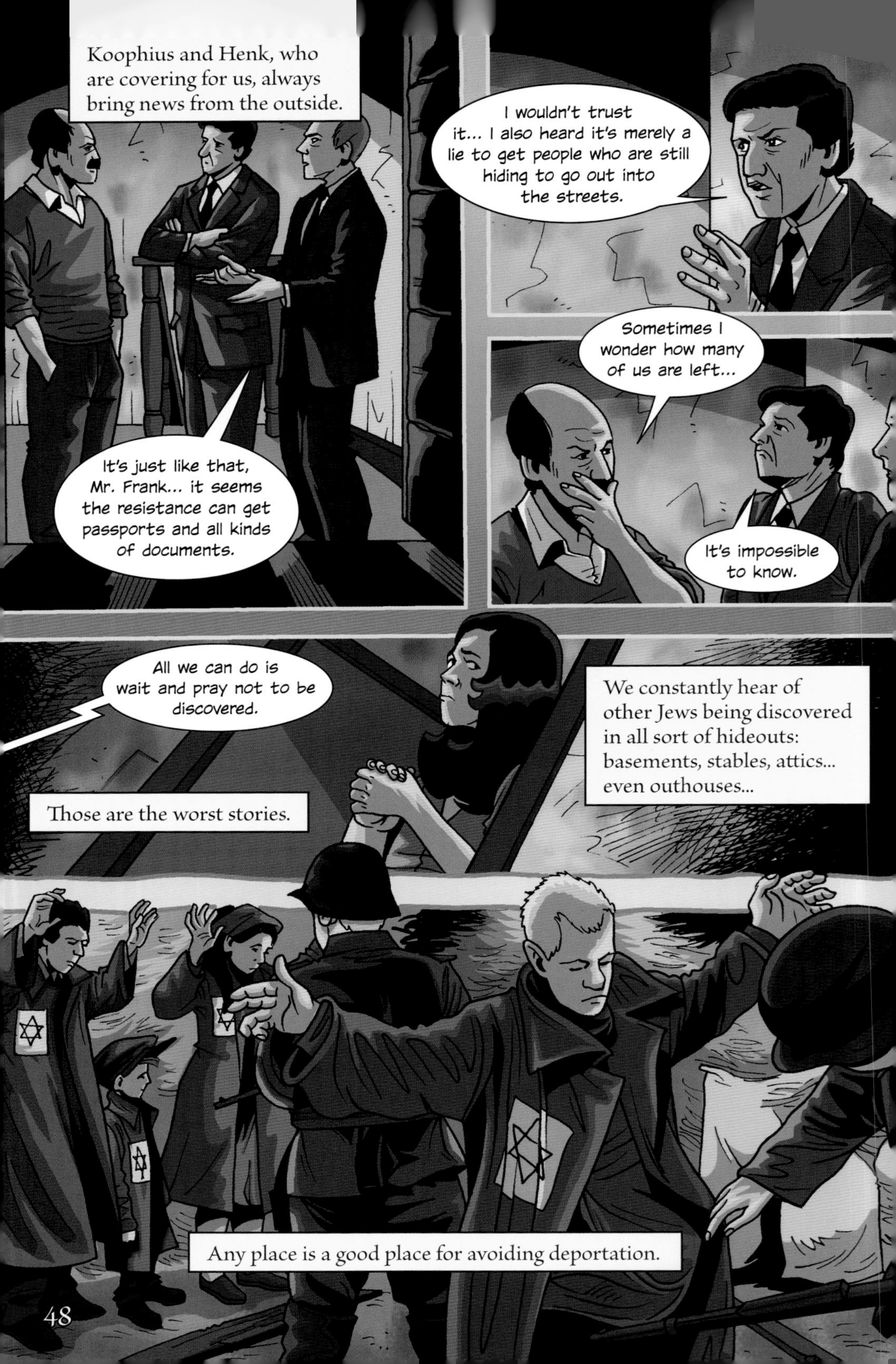
Koophius and Henk, who are covering for us, always bring news from the outside.
It's just like that, Mr. Frank... it seems the resistance can get passports and all kinds of documents.
I wouldn't trust it... I also heard it's merely a lie to get people who are still hiding to go out into the streets.
Sometimes I wonder how many of us are left...
It's impossible to know.
All we can do is wait and pray not to be discovered.
We constantly hear of other Jews being discovered in all sort of hideouts: basements, stables, attics... even outhouses...
Those are the worst stories.
Any place is a good place for avoiding deportation.

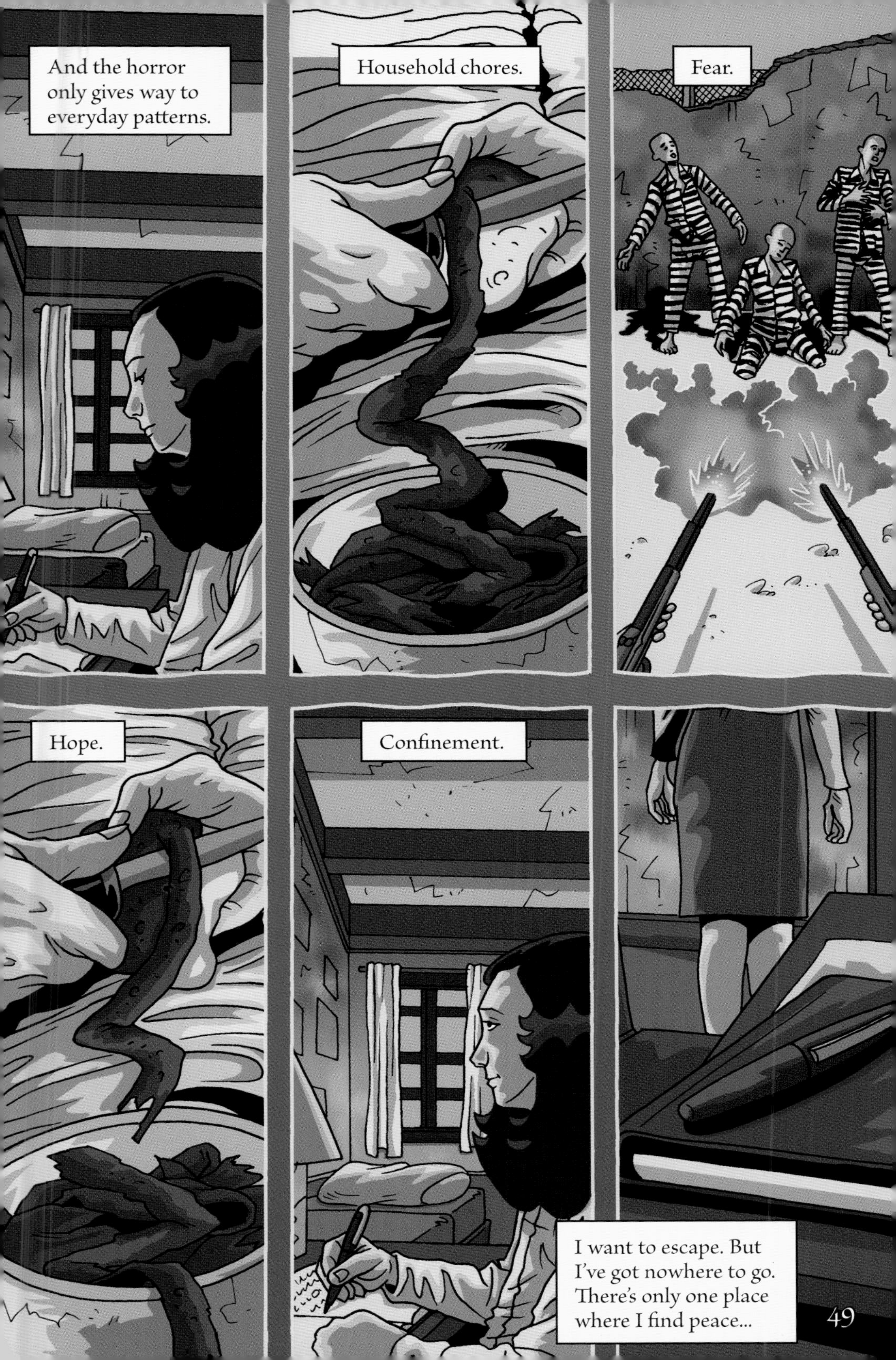

And the horror only gives way to everyday patterns.
Household chores.
Fear.
Hope.
Confinement.
I want to escape. But I've got nowhere to go. There's only one place where I find peace...

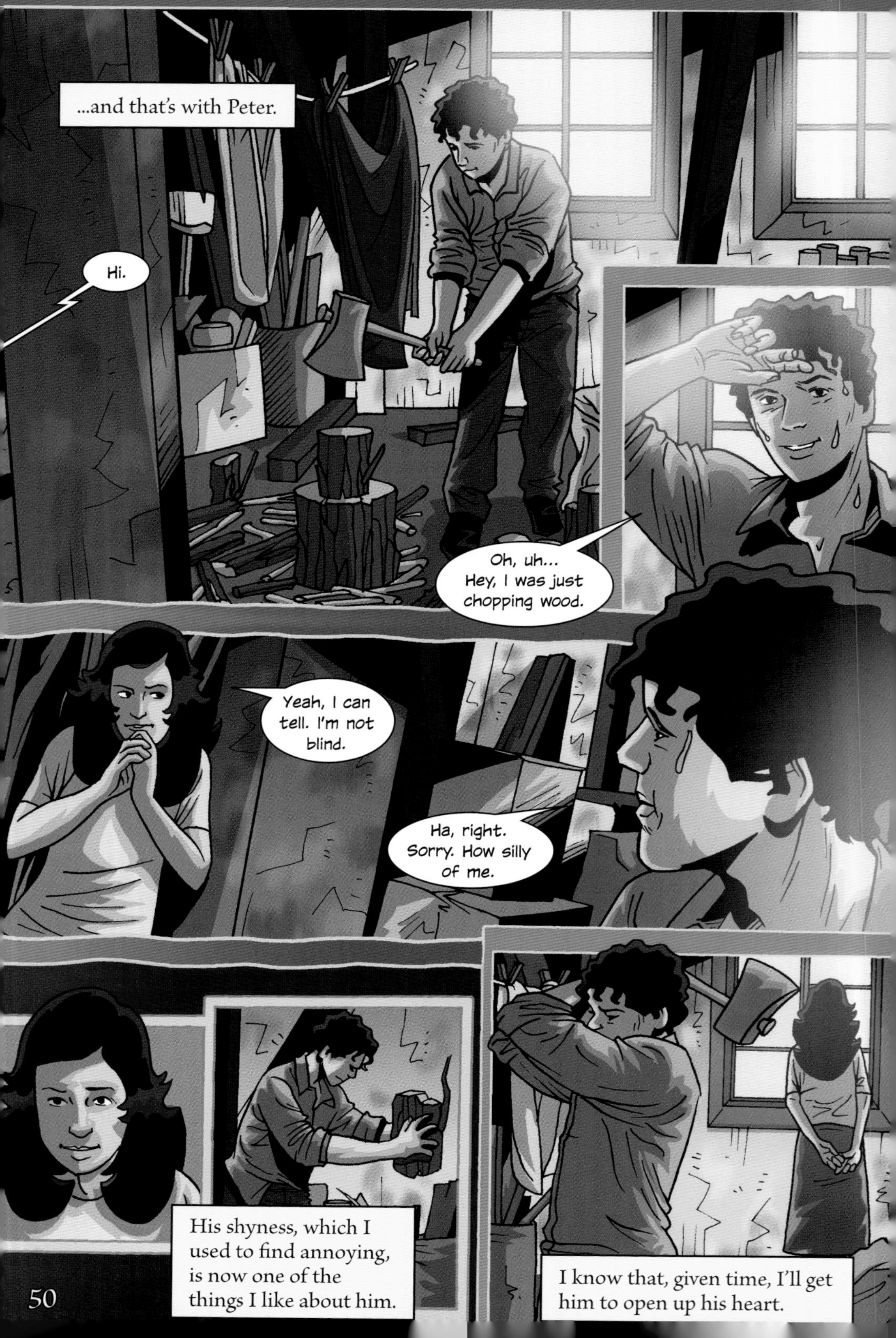
...and that's with Peter.
Hi.
Oh, uh...
Hey, I was just chopping wood.
Yeah, I can tell. I'm not blind.
Ha, right. Sorry. How silly of me.
His shyness, which I used to find annoying, is now one of the things I like about him.
I know that, given time, I'll get him to open up his heart.

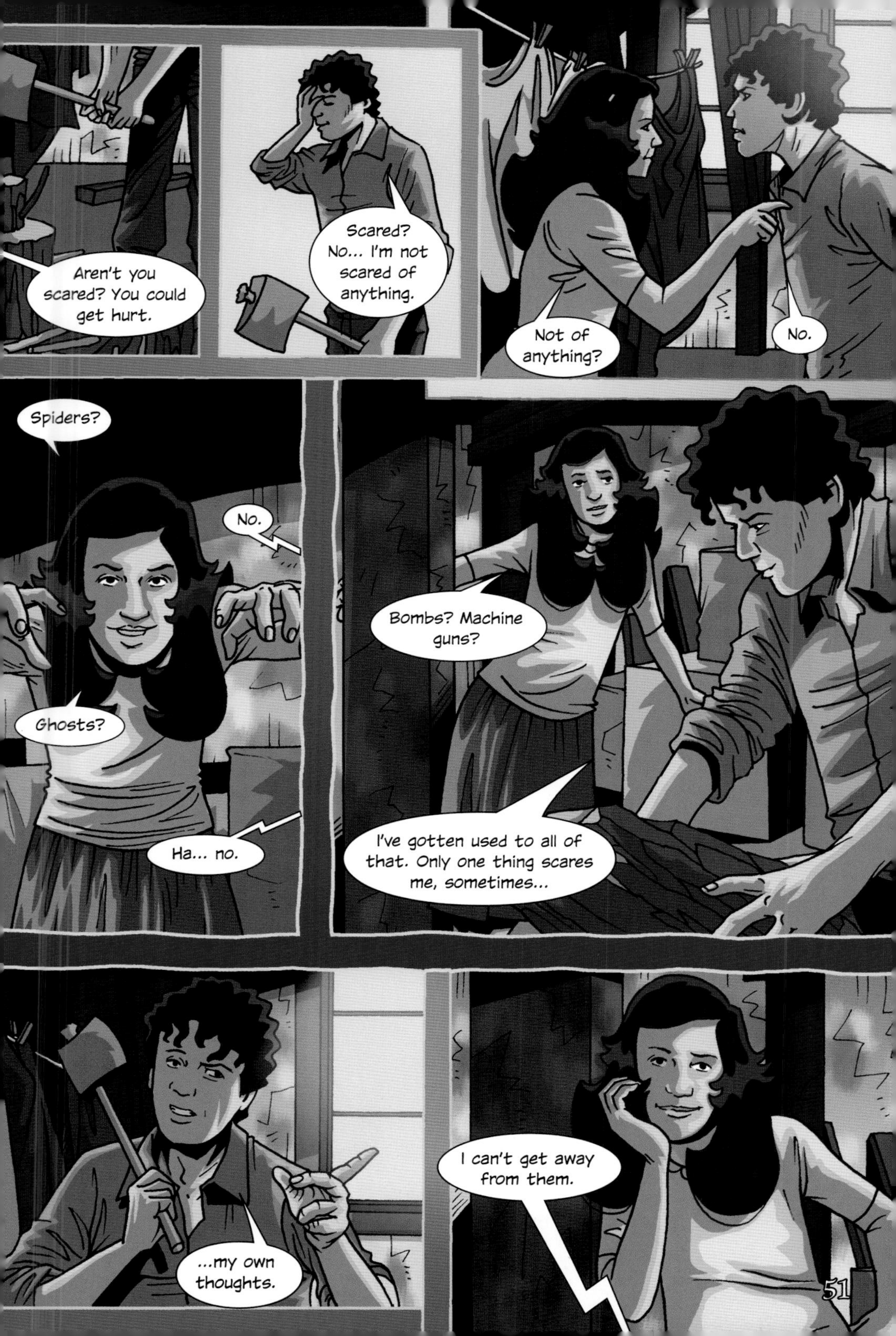
Aren't you scared? You could get hurt.
Scared? No... I'm not scared of anything.
Not of anything?
No.
Spiders?
No.
Ghosts?
Ha... no.
Bombs? Machine guns?
I've gotten used to all of that. Only one thing scares me, sometimes...
...my own thoughts.
I can't get away from them.

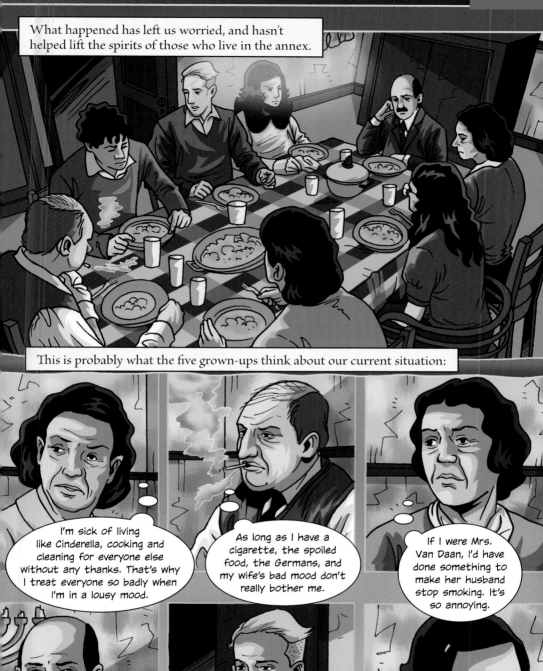

What happened has left us worried, and hasn't helped lift the spirits of those who live in the annex.

This is probably what the five grown-ups think about our current situation:

I'm sick of living like Cinderella, cooking and cleaning for everyone else without any thanks. That's why I treat everyone so badly when I'm in a lousy mood.

As long as I have a cigarette, the spoiled food, the Germans, and my wife's bad mood don't really bother me.

If I were Mrs. Van Daan, I'd have done something to make her husband stop smoking. It's so annoying.

Everything's fine, and I don't need anything. A little more patience, that's all. We can hold on while we still have potatoes.

I only want to finish my research on time. They'll never catch us, so why worry?

Why can't I have a say? It's my safety too!

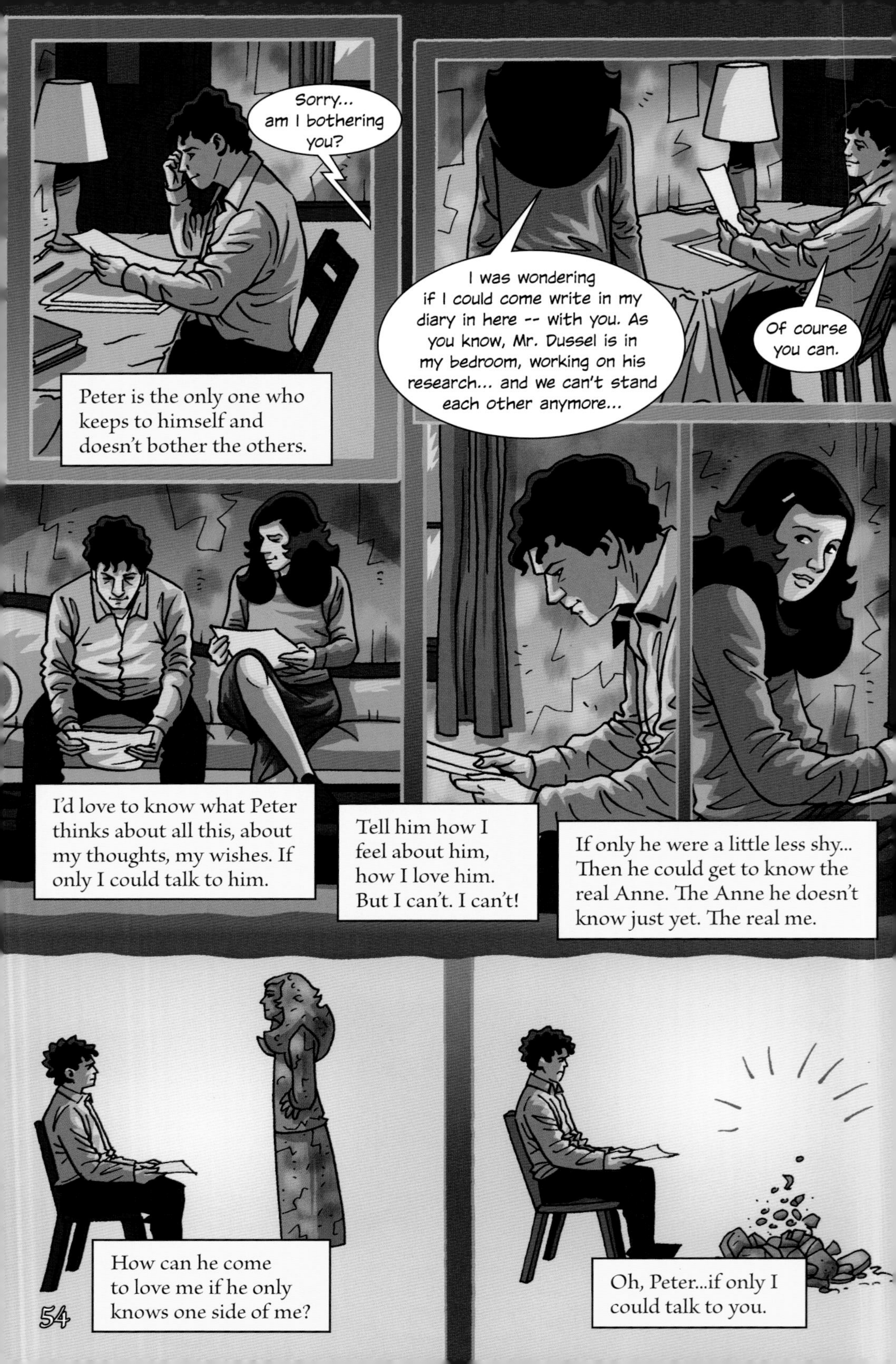
Sorry... am I bothering you?
Peter is the only one who keeps to himself and doesn't bother the others.
I was wondering if I could come write in my diary in here -- with you. As you know, Mr. Dussel is in my bedroom, working on his research... and we can't stand each other anymore...
Of course you can.
I'd love to know what Peter thinks about all this, about my thoughts, my wishes. If only I could talk to him.
Tell him how I feel about him, how I love him. But I can't. I can't!
If only he were a little less shy... Then he could get to know the real Anne. The Anne he doesn't know just yet. The real me.
How can he come to love me if he only knows one side of me?
Oh, Peter...if only I could talk to you.

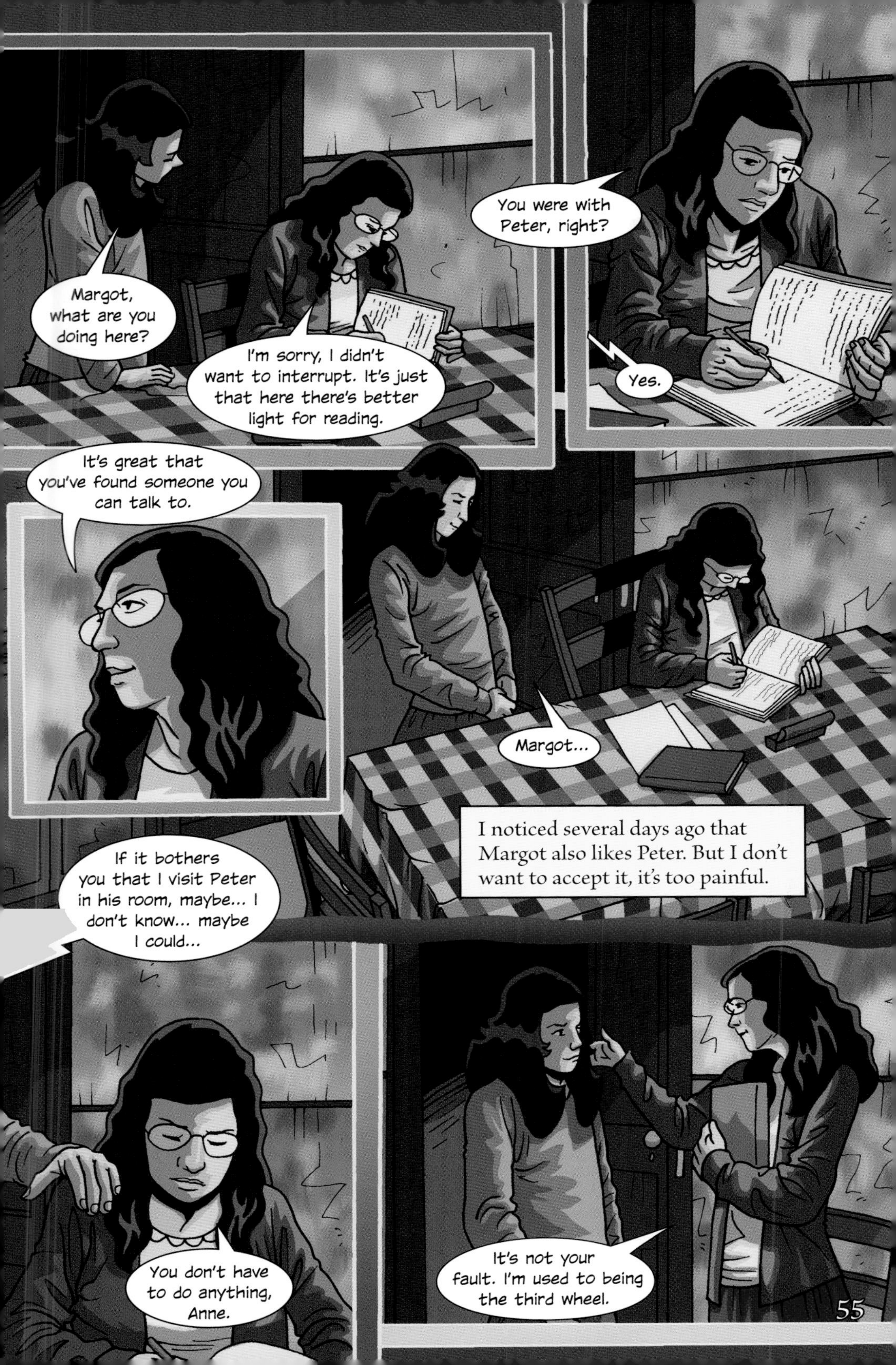
Margot, what are you doing here?
I'm sorry, I didn't want to interrupt. It's just that here there's better light for reading.
You were with Peter, right?
Yes.
It's great that you've found someone you can talk to.
Margot...
I noticed several days ago that Margot also likes Peter. But I don't want to accept it, it's too painful.
If it bothers you that I visit Peter in his room, maybe... I don't know... maybe I could...
You don't have to do anything, Anne.
It's not your fault. I'm used to being the third wheel.

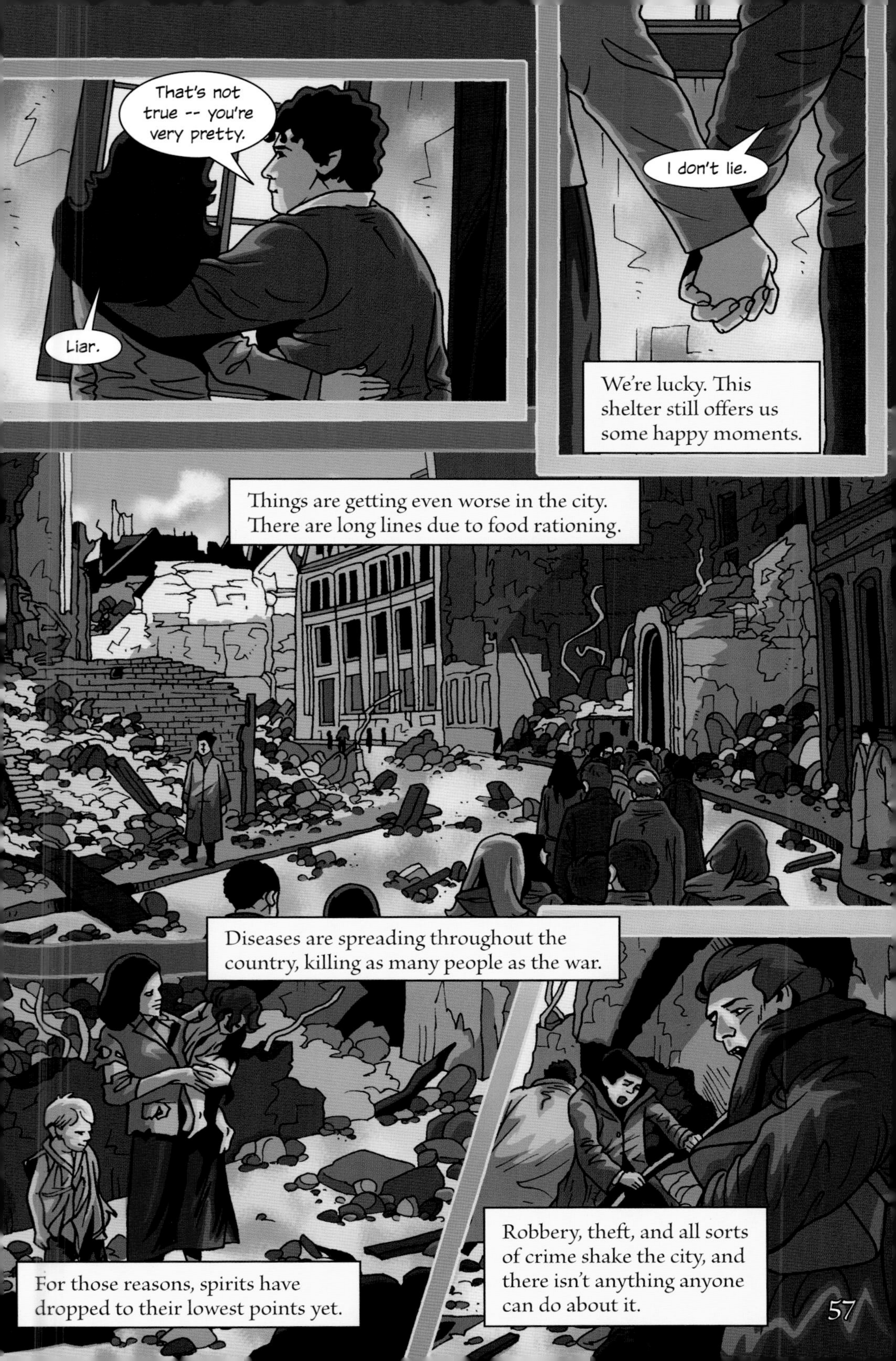
That's not true -- you're very pretty.
Liar.
I don't lie.
We're lucky. This shelter still offers us some happy moments.
Things are getting even worse in the city. There are long lines due to food rationing.
Diseases are spreading throughout the country, killing as many people as the war.
For those reasons, spirits have dropped to their lowest points yet.
Robbery, theft, and all sorts of crime shake the city, and there isn't anything anyone can do about it.

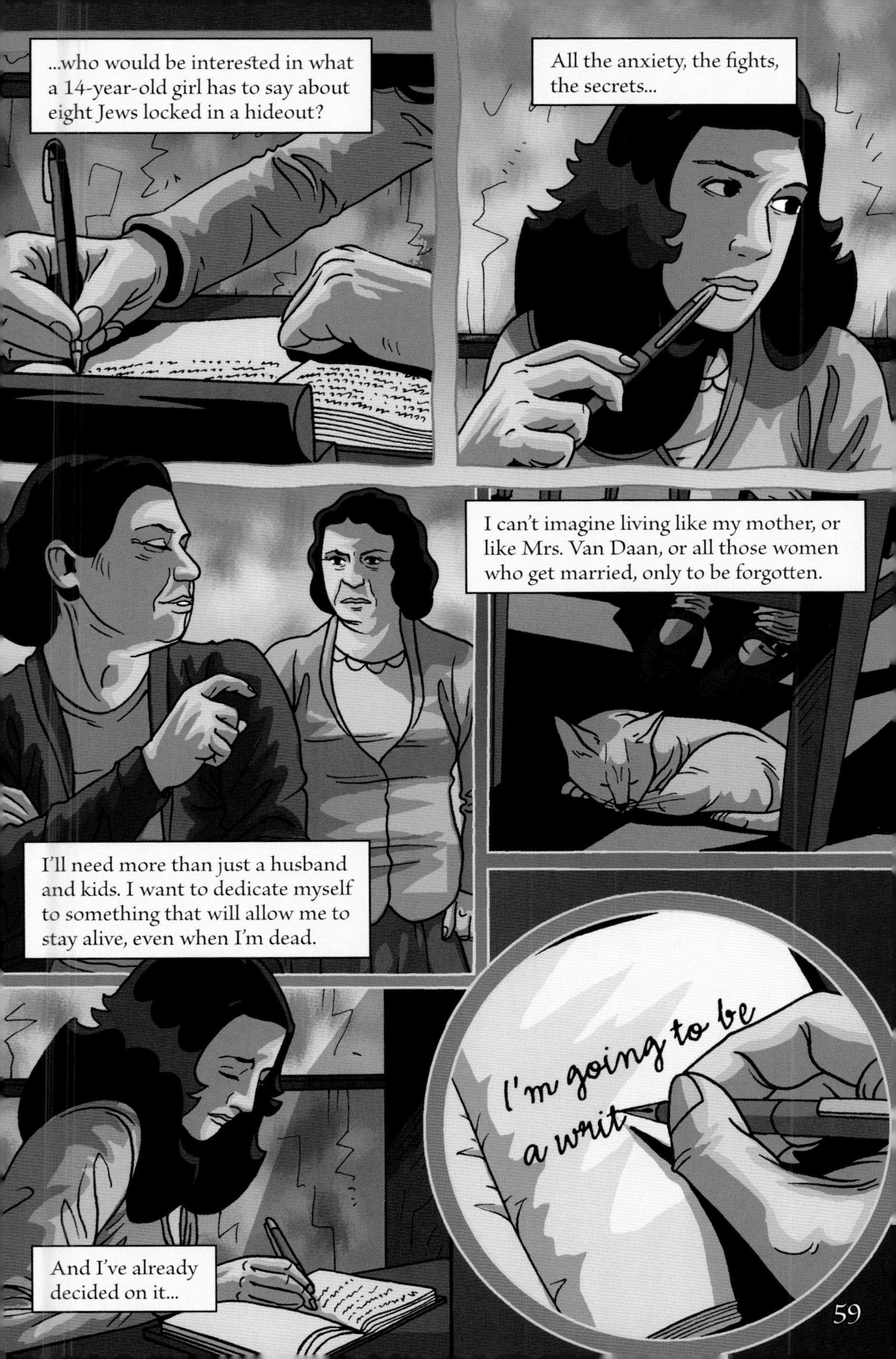

...who would be interested in what a 14-year-old girl has to say about eight Jews locked in a hideout?
All the anxiety, the fights, the secrets...
I can't imagine living like my mother, or like Mrs. Van Daan, or all those women who get married, only to be forgotten.
I'll need more than just a husband and kids. I want to dedicate myself to something that will allow me to stay alive, even when I'm dead.
And I've already decided on it...
I'm going to be a writ

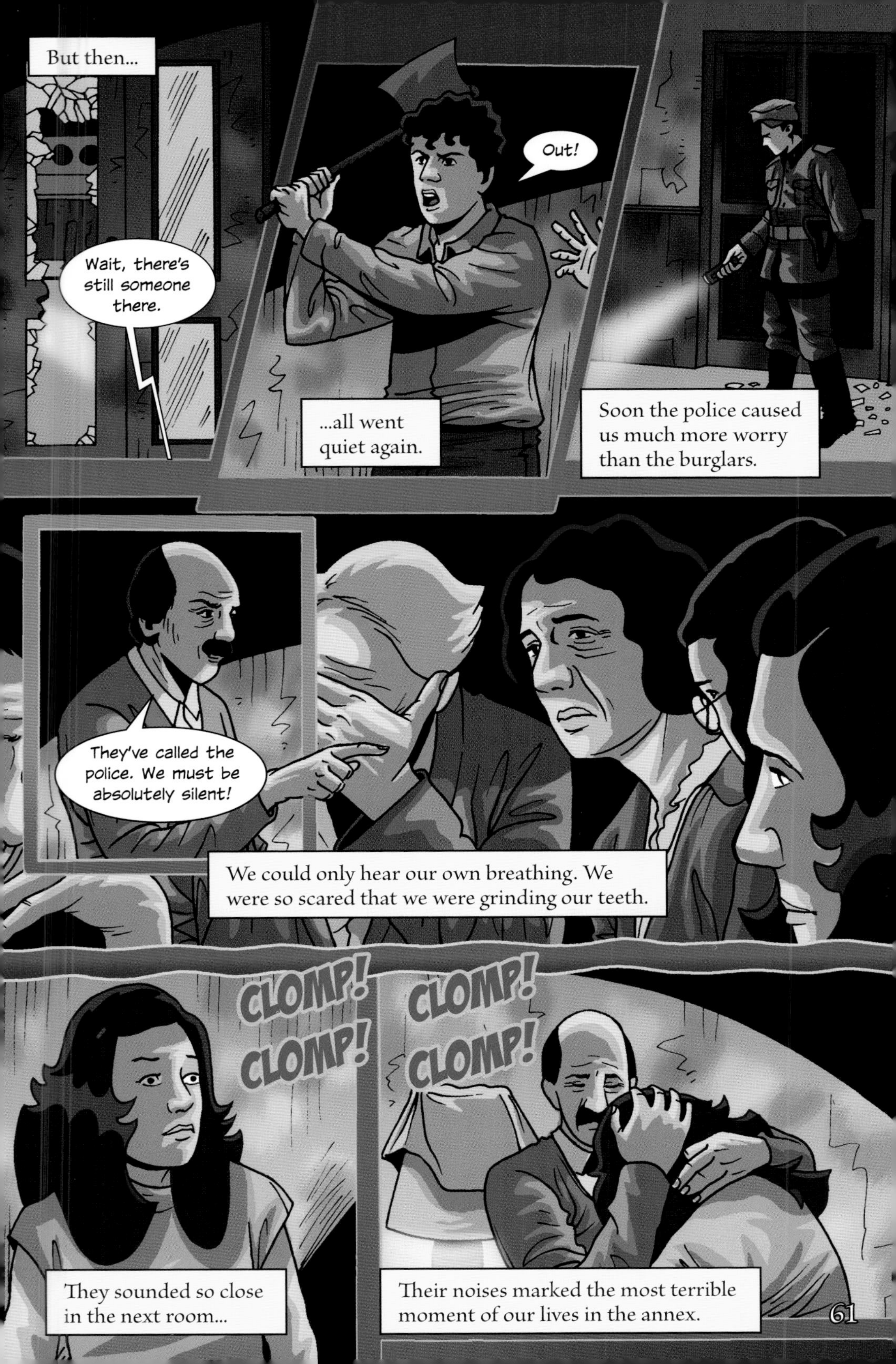

But then...
Wait, there's still someone there.
Out!
...all went quiet again.
Soon the police caused us much more worry than the burglars.
They've called the police. We must be absolutely silent!
We could only hear our own breathing. We were so scared that we were grinding our teeth.
CLOMP! CLOMP!
CLOMP! CLOMP!
They sounded so close in the next room...
Their noises marked the most terrible moment of our lives in the annex.

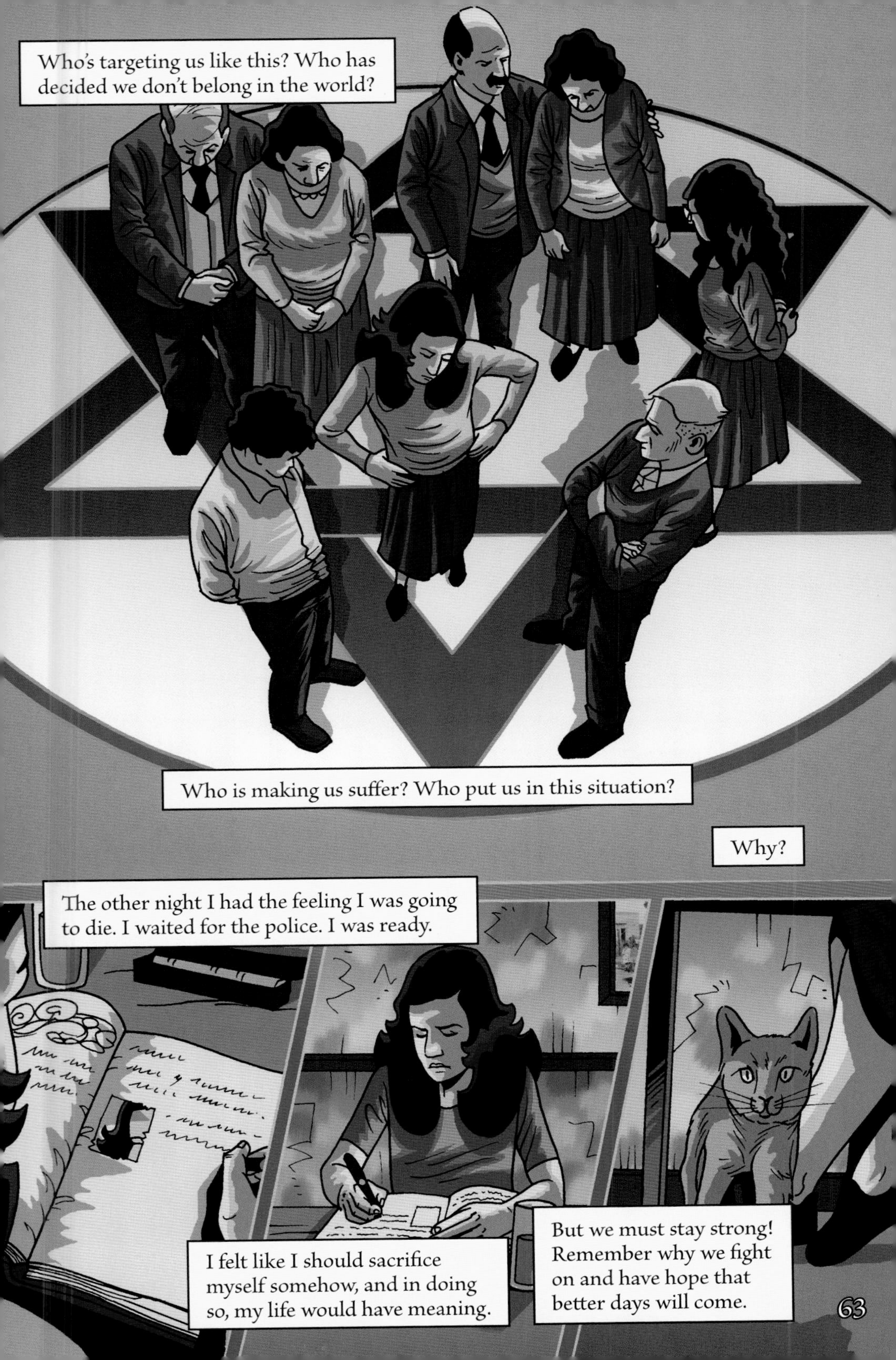

Who's targeting us like this? Who has decided we don't belong in the world?
Who is making us suffer? Who put us in this situation?
Why?
The other night I had the feeling I was going to die. I waited for the police. I was ready.
I felt like I should sacrifice myself somehow, and in doing so, my life would have meaning.
But we must stay strong! Remember why we fight on and have hope that better days will come.

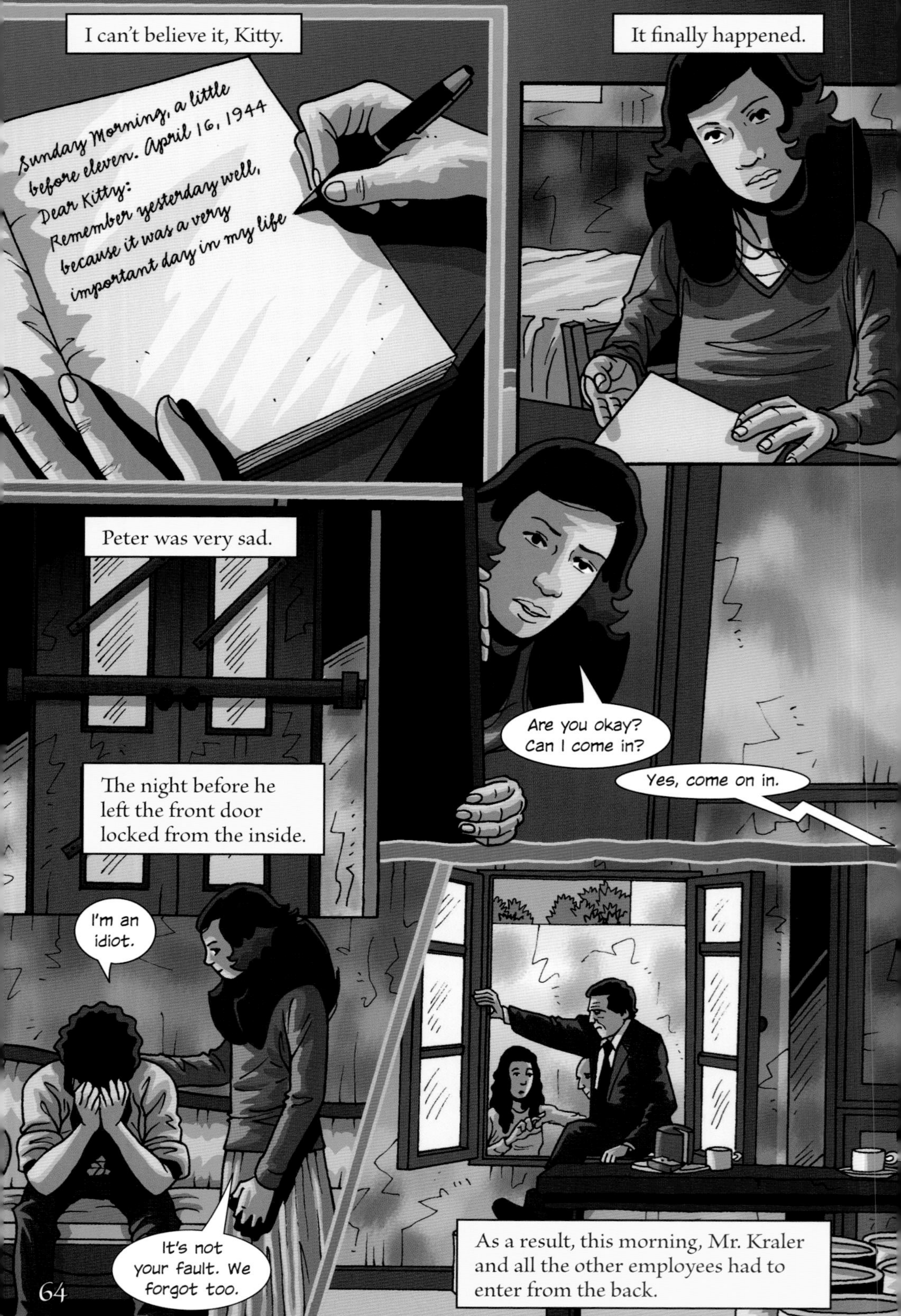
I can't believe it, Kitty.
Sunday Morning, a little before eleven. April 16, 1944
Dear Kitty:
Remember yesterday well, because it was a very important day in my life
It finally happened.
Peter was very sad.
Are you okay? Can I come in?
Yes, come on in.
The night before he left the front door locked from the inside.
I'm an idiot.
It's not your fault. We forgot too.
As a result, this morning, Mr. Kraler and all the other employees had to enter from the back.

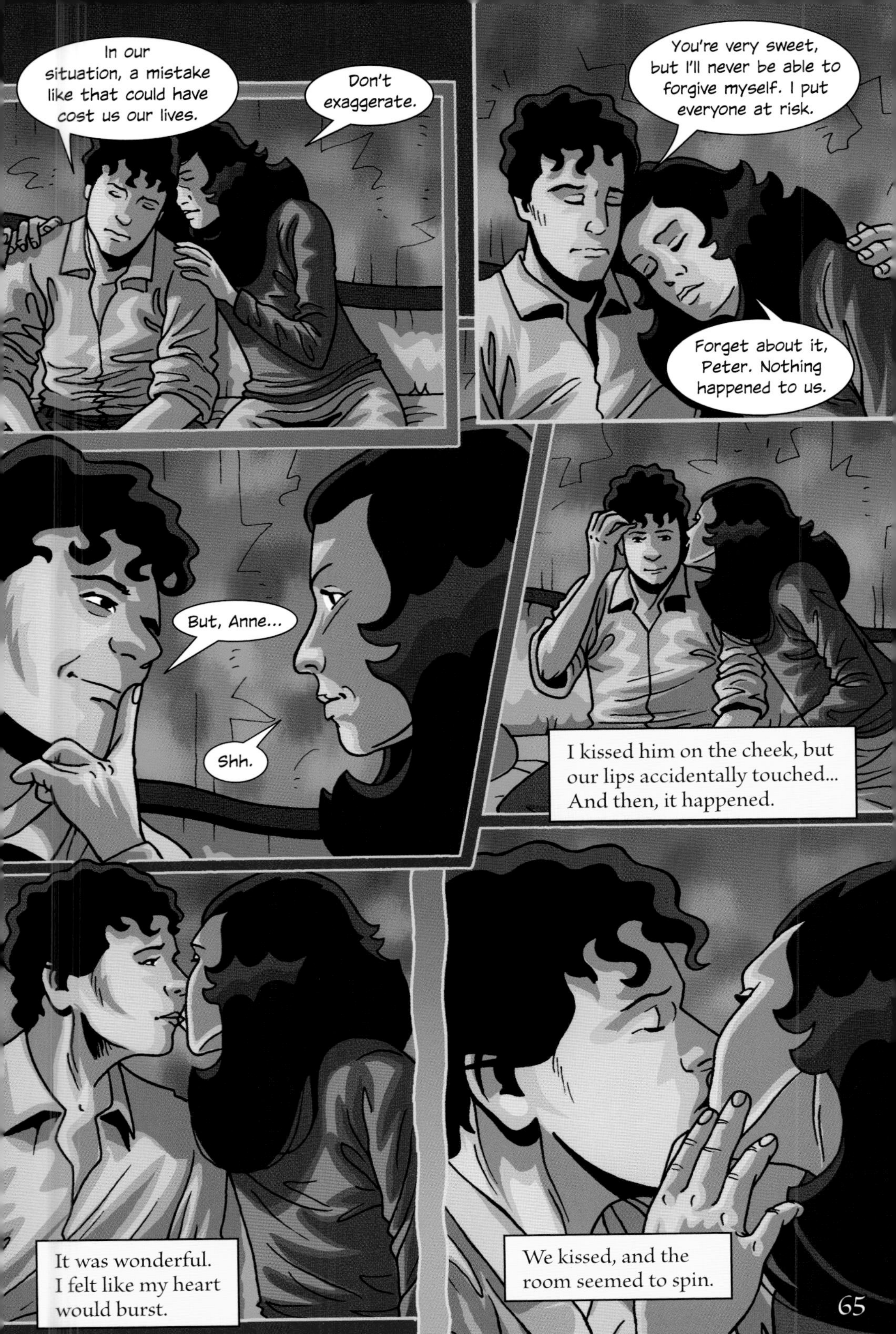
In our situation, a mistake like that could have cost us our lives.
Don't exaggerate.
You're very sweet, but I'll never be able to forgive myself. I put everyone at risk.
Forget about it, Peter. Nothing happened to us.
But, Anne...
Shh.
I kissed him on the cheek, but our lips accidentally touched... And then, it happened.
It was wonderful. I felt like my heart would burst.
We kissed, and the room seemed to spin.

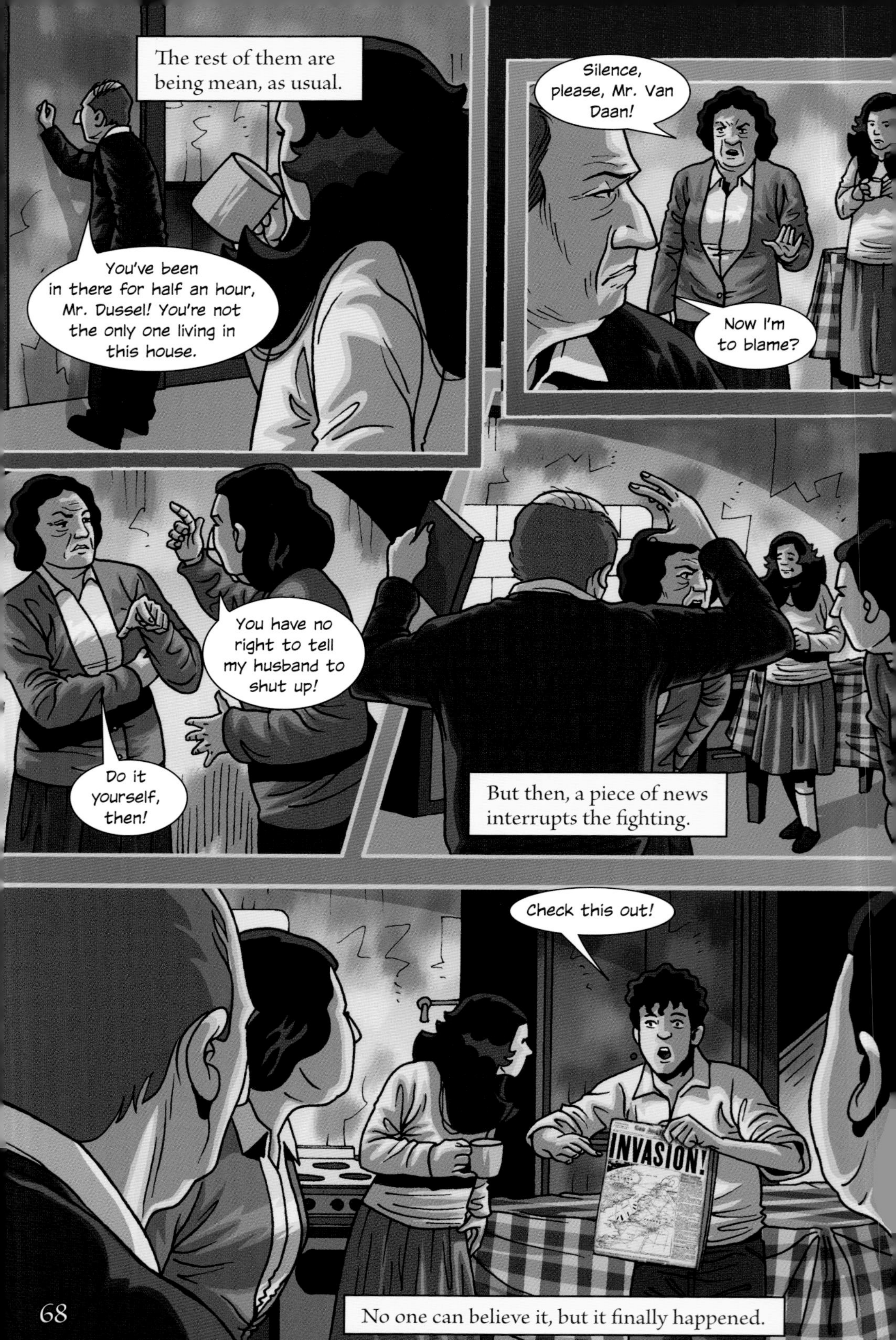
The rest of them are being mean, as usual.
You've been in there for half an hour, Mr. Dussel! You're not the only one living in this house.
Silence, please, Mr. Van Daan!
Now I'm to blame?
You have no right to tell my husband to shut up!
Do it yourself, then!
But then, a piece of news interrupts the fighting.
Check this out!
INVASION!
No one can believe it, but it finally happened.

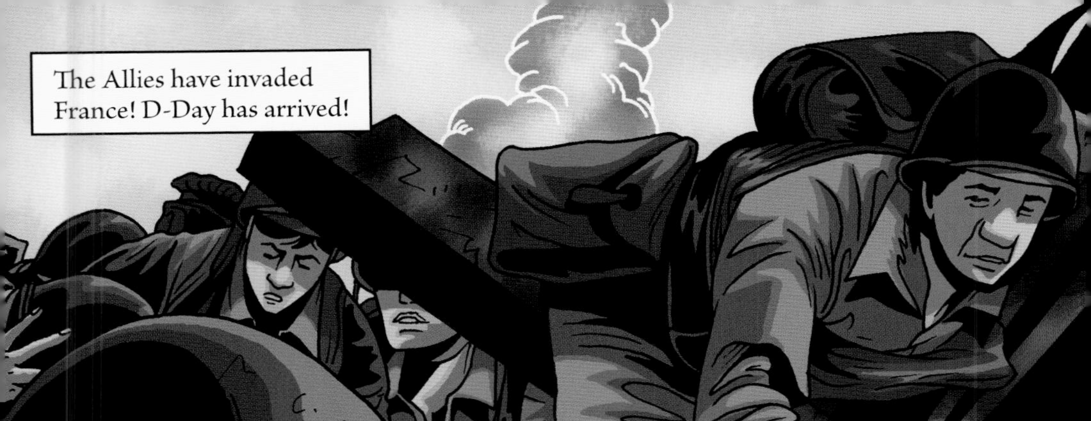
The Allies have invaded France! D-Day has arrived!
The troops have left Normandy!

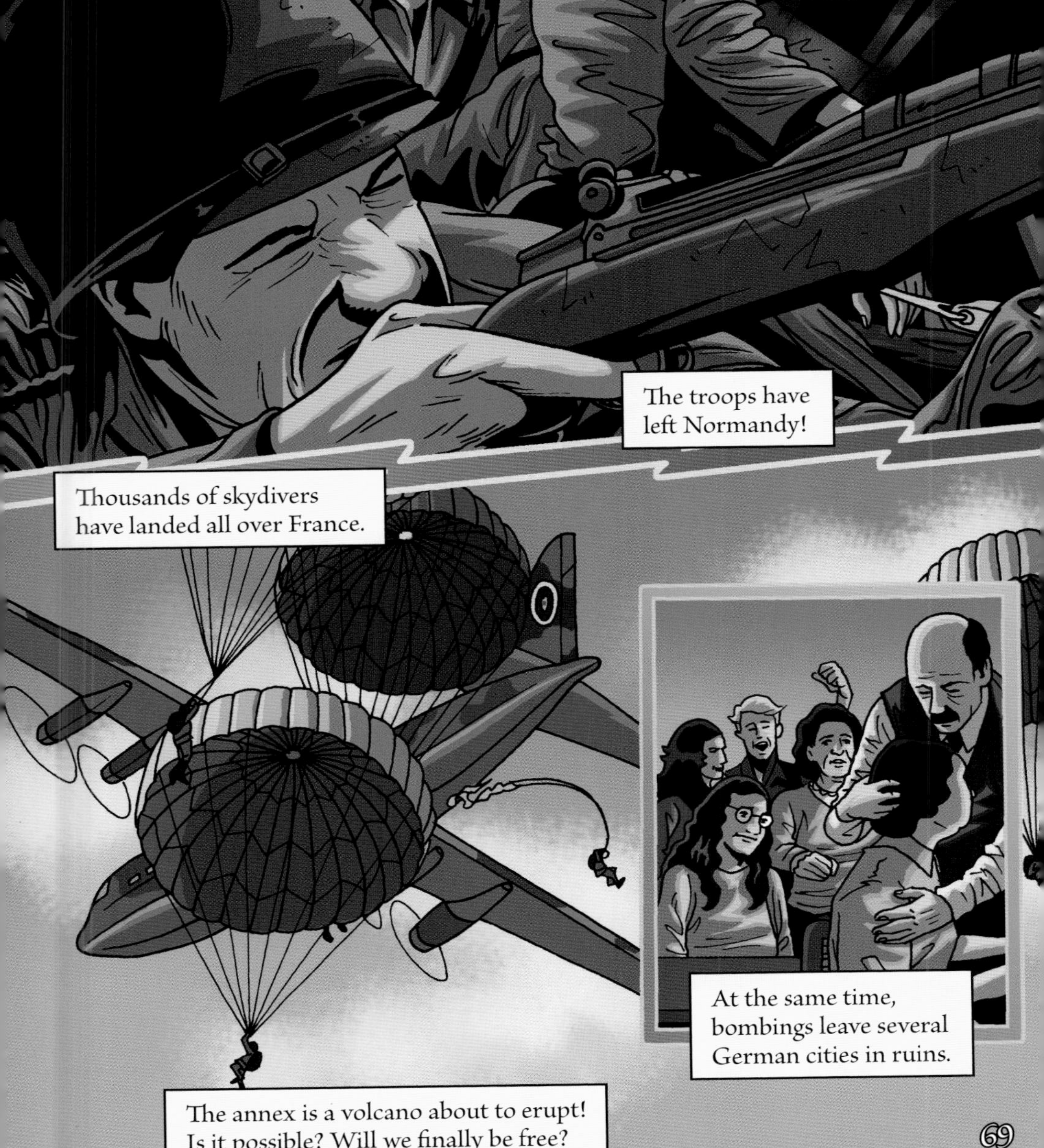
Thousands of skydivers have landed all over France.
At the same time, bombings leave several German cities in ruins.
The annex is a volcano about to erupt! Is it possible? Will we finally be free?

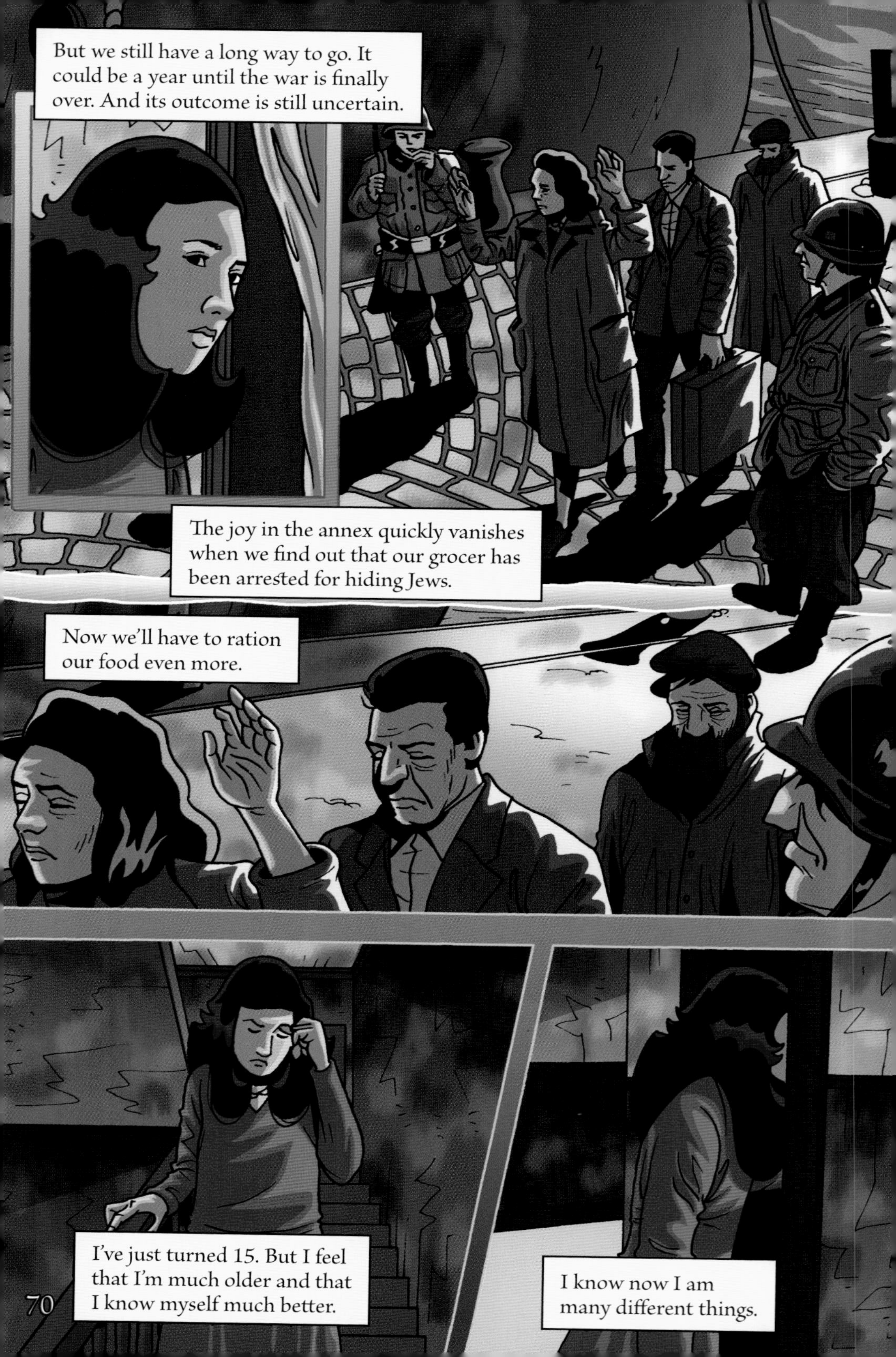
But we still have a long way to go. It could be a year until the war is finally over. And its outcome is still uncertain.
The joy in the annex quickly vanishes when we find out that our grocer has been arrested for hiding Jews.
Now we'll have to ration our food even more.
I've just turned 15. But I feel that I'm much older and that I know myself much better.
I know now I am many different things.

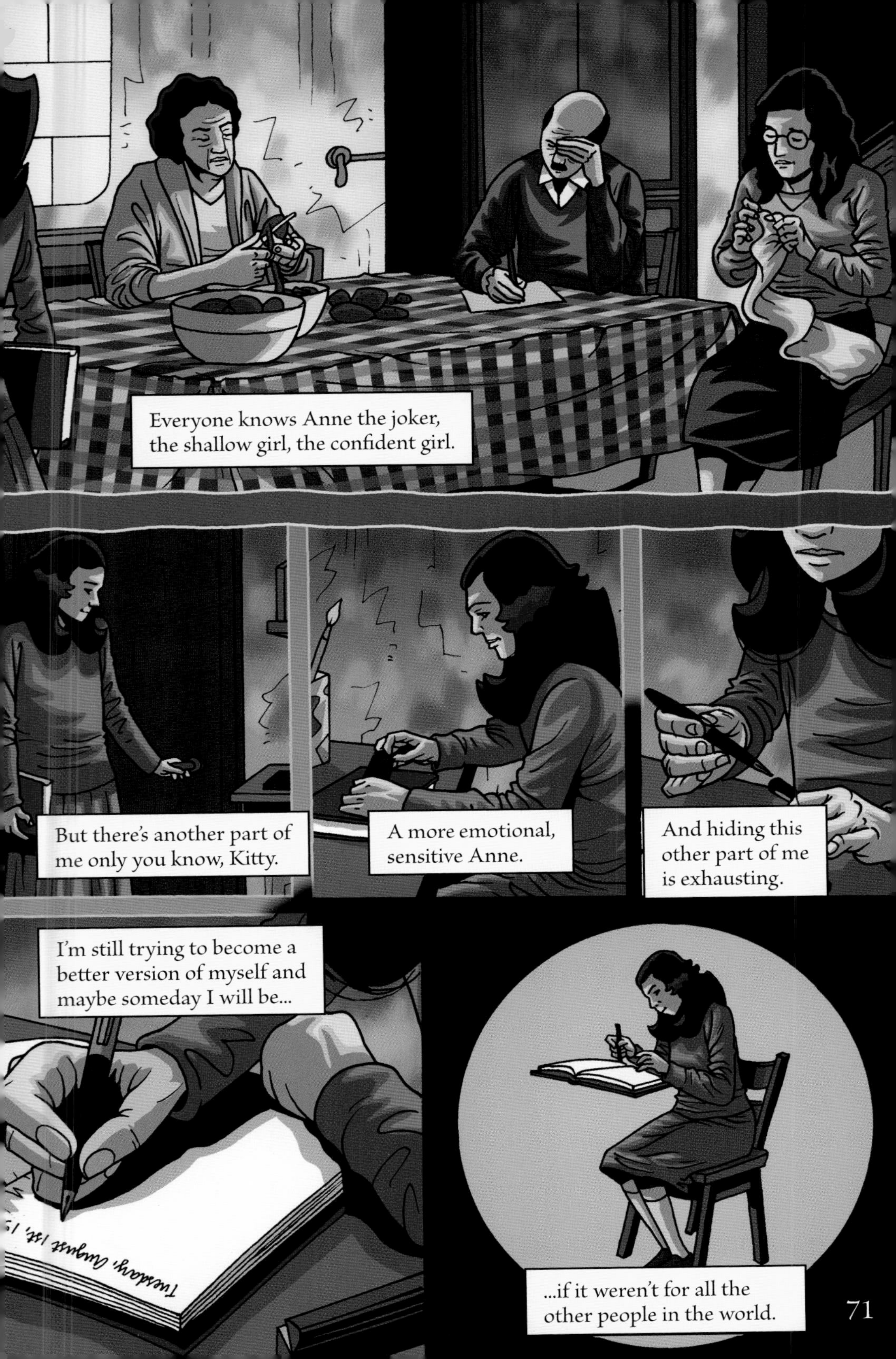
Everyone knows Anne the joker, the shallow girl, the confident girl.
But there's another part of me only you know, Kitty.
A more emotional, sensitive Anne.
And hiding this other part of me is exhausting.
I'm still trying to become a better version of myself and maybe someday I will be...
Tuesday, August 1st,
...if it weren't for all the other people in the world.

ANNE FRANK'S STORY: A LEGACY

When Adolf Hitler, leader of the National Socialist Workers' Party, or the Nazi's, became leader of Germany in 1933, the Frank family could imagine that difficult times would come. This totalitarian party was anti-Semitic, which means it hated Jews. That caused a drastic change in the daily life of all German Jews.

Among other things, the government increasingly restricted the daily lives of Jews, such as assigning specific places for transit or recreation, separate from the rest of the Germans. Jews soon became victims of the Holocaust, the systematic persecution and extermination plan carried out in different concentration camps. This situation continued and worsened during World War II (1939–1945). During the war, Germany occupied several countries, among them Poland and Holland. There, the Nazis captured all Jews. This included the Frank family and their companions, the Van Pels and Mr. Pfeffer (who appear in Anne's diary as the Van Daans and Mr. Dussel), who were discovered in August 1944, after two years of hiding.

In 1945, after the Soviets liberated Auschwitz, one of the cruelest concentration camps, Otto Frank returned to Amsterdam. He soon learned of the death of his entire family. Later, Miep Gies, one of the Franks' loyal protectors while they were in hiding, gave him Anne's diary. It was the only thing left in the house after the arrest. Two years later, Otto fulfilled Anne's wishes and published her diary. It was titled *The Secret Annex*, just as Anne had wished.

After the diary's publication, Otto received and answered many letters from Anne's readers. This work, and his ongoing fight for human rights around the world, continued until his death. The diary became a testament to the Holocaust and was translated into 67 languages.

"The back house," or "the annex," was transformed into a museum thanks to Otto's efforts to preserve and restore it. In 1960, it opened to the public under the name the "Anne Frank House." Today, almost one million people visit it every year. Those who visit can tour the rooms and take part in different activities and workshops. These activities are designed to promote respect for human rights and warn about the dangers of anti-Semitism, racism, and discrimination. In 2010, on the museum's 50th anniversary, Anne's writings were exhibited to the public.

ABOUT ANNE FRANK

Anne Frank was born in 1929 in Frankfurt, Germany. She lived with her parents, Otto and Edith, and her older sister, Margot. With Hitler's rise to power in 1933, they had to leave for Amsterdam. After the beginning of World War II, Holland was invaded by Germany, and the Frank family found itself in danger again. They decided to hide in a secret house behind Otto Frank's office. That same year, Anne received a diary as a birthday gift, a diary she would fill with her experiences and thoughts. In 1944, the residents of the hideout were betrayed by some of their Dutch neighbors and arrested by the Gestapo. They were deported from Holland, and both Anne and her sister were sent to the Bergen-Belsen concentration camp. In March 1945, shortly before the camp was liberated and the war was over, they both died of typhus fever. Otto Frank was the only surviving family member.

ANNE FRANK AND THE MOVIES

In 1959, *The Diary of Anne Frank* made its debut. It was a movie based on a theater play of the same name. Even though the film wasn't a box office hit, it received three Academy Awards, or Oscars. It was one of the first Hollywood movies to tackle the persecution of Jews. Since then, the Holocaust has been featured in more than 20 feature films and documentaries.

Schindler's List was directed by Steven Spielberg in 1993, based on the novel *Schindler's Ark*, by Thomas Keneally. It tells the story of Oskar Schindler, a German businessman who sheltered a thousand Jews in his factory, saving them from the Holocaust. This movie received multiple awards, including seven Oscars.

Life Is Beautiful is a famous 1997 Italian movie set in 1939. It tells the tender yet sad story of the imaginary games that Guido, a Jewish Italian man, makes up so that his son, Giosué, can handle, and finally survive, life in a concentration camp. This movie is based on a book written by an Auschwitz survivor.

In 2002, Roman Polanski brought *The Pianist* to the movie screen. It tells the story of Wladyslaw Szpilman, a Polish pianist and composer who survived both the Warsaw ghetto and World War II. His memoir, *The Pianist: The Extraordinary Story of One Man's Survival in Warsaw, 1939–45*, is one of many horrible tales depicting the Holocaust. In it, Szpilman recounts his life and how he escapes death after being discovered by a German officer. The officer asked him to play a Chopin piece in exchange for letting him live. The movie received many awards, including three Oscars.

GLOSSARY

Allied forces (AL-ide FORSS-ess)—countries united against Germany during World War II, including France, the United States, Canada, Great Britain, and others

annex (AN-eks)—an extra building that is joined onto or placed near a main building

arrogant (A-ruh-guhnt)—exaggerating one's own self-worth or importance, often in an overbearing manner

atmosphere (AT-muhss-fihr)—a mood or feeling of a place

BBC (BBC)—British Broadcasting Corporation; a British public service broadcaster that produces radio and TV shows

chamber pot (CHAYM-buhr POT)—a type of bowl that people used as a toilet

concentration camp (kahn-suhn-TRAY-shuhn KAMP)—a place where thousands of people are held under harsh conditions

confrontational (kuhn-FRUHN-tay-shuhn-uhl)—acting in a threatening way, usually to argue with someone else

defend (di-FEND)—to try to keep someone or something from being harmed

deport (di-PORT)—to send people back to their own country

extermination (ek-STUR-muh-nay-shuhn)—killing or destroying someone or something

gas chamber (GASS CHAYM-buhr)—a room where people are killed with poison gas

Gestapo (guh-STAH-poh)—the secret police of Nazi Germany; the Gestapo is a subdivision of the SS

interrupt (in-tuh-RUHPT)—to get in the way of someone

loyal (LOY-uhl)—being true to something or someone

Nazi (NOT-see)—a member of a political party led by Adolf Hitler; the Nazis ruled Germany from 1933 to 1945

orphan (OR-fuhn)—a child whose parents have died

persecution (PUR-suh-kyoo-shuhn)—cruel or unfair treatment, often because of race or religious beliefs

ration (RASH-uhn)—to limit to prevent running out of something

retired (rih-TIRED)—a person who has given up work usually because of his or her age

socialize (SOH-shuh-lize)—to get together or talk with other people in a friendly way

support (suh-PORT)—to help and encourage someone

tolerant (TOL-ur-uhnt)—able to put up with something

totalitarian (toh-tayl-uh-TEHR-ee-uhn)—of or relating to a political system in which the government has complete control over the people

DISCUSSION QUESTIONS

1. Why do you think Anne Frank's story has touched so many readers?

2. Mrs. Van Daan thinks Anne is a spoiled child. Do you agree? Explain your answer.

3. Do you think you could live a long time locked inside your home? Why or why not?

WRITING PROMPTS

1. Anne Frank described most of her everyday life while she was locked up in the secret annex. What do you think a day in your life would be like if you were locked in your home? What would you do and what wouldn't you do? Write a letter to a friend describing your experience.

2. Anne received her diary when she was thirteen, which helped her realize that she wanted to be a writer. Write a paragraph describing one of your favorite gifts. What makes it so special?

3. Imagine if the Frank family hadn't been arrested and instead was able to leave their hideout in peace. Pretend you're Anne. Write a diary entry about the first thing you would have done once you left the annex.

ABOUT THE AUTHOR

Diego Agrimbau, from Buenos Aires, Argentina, has written more than a dozen graphic novels for various publishing houses around the world. He has won multiple awards, among them the 2005 Prix Utopiales for *Bertold's Bubble*, the 2009 Premio Planeta DeAgostini for Comic Books for *Planet Extra*, and the 2011 Premio Dibujando entre Culturas for *The Desert Robots*. He's currently a contributor to *Fierro* magazine and writes "Los Canillitas" comic scripts for the newspaper *Tiempo Argentino*.

ABOUT THE ILLUSTRATOR

Fabián Mezquita, from Argentina, started publishing his work in 1998. In 2001, he worked for a year as an assistant, and then continued his career as an illustrator, working for ad agencies and various publishing houses, both in Argentina and abroad. He is a founding and active member of Banda Dibujada, a cultural organization created to promote comic books for children and young adults.

READ MORE

Hollingsworth, Tamara. *Anne Frank: A Light in the Dark.* Huntington Beach, Cali.: Teacher Created Materials, 2013.

Hurwitz, Johanna. *Anne Frank: Life in Hiding.* Lincoln, Neb.: University of Nebraska Press, 2014.

Killcoyne, Hope Lourie. *Anne Frank: Heroic Diarist of the Holocaust.* Britannica Beginner Bios. New York: Britannica Educational Publishing, 2016.

INTERNET SITES

Use Facthound to find Internet sites related to this book.

Visit *www.facthound.com*

Just type in 9781515791614 and go!

 **Super-cool stuff!** Check out projects, games and lots more at **www.capstonekids.com**

INDEX